WHISKEY IN A TEACUP

WHAT GROWING UP IN THE SOUTH TAUGHT ME
ABOUT LIFE, LOVE AND BAKING BISCUITS

REESE WITHERSPOON

SIMON &
SCHUSTER

London · New York · Sydney · Toronto · New Delhi

A CBS COMPANY

First published in the United States by Touchstone,
an imprint of Simon & Schuster, Inc., 2018
First published in Great Britain by Simon & Schuster UK Ltd, 2018
A CBS COMPANY

1 3 5 7 9 10 8 6 4 2

Simon & Schuster UK Ltd
1st Floor
222 Gray's Inn Road
London WC1X 8HB

www.simonandschuster.co.uk
www.simonandschuster.com.au
www.simonandschuster.co.in

Simon & Schuster Australia, Sydney
Simon & Schuster India, New Delhi

Interior design by Jennifer K. Beal Davis
Jacket design by Jennifer K. Beal Davis
Cover photography by Paul Costello

A CIP catalogue record for this book
is available from the British Library

Hardback ISBN: 978-1-4711-6622-8
eBook ISBN: 978-1-4711-6623-5

Printed in Italy

WHISKEY IN A TEACUP

For my children, Ava, Deacon,
and Tennessee.
I hope they always think of me
when they hear a Dolly Parton song.

⸻

And for my grandmother
Dorothea and grandfather Jimmy.
Thanks to you, I'm a good friend
and a good cook, and I never
wear sweatpants on airplanes.

CONT

ENTS

Whiskey in a Teacup

In my late twenties, I found myself facing some hard choices. I'd enjoyed a great deal of success in movies, but personally, I was at a crossroads. I didn't know where I was going to find the strength to pick a path. One particularly rough day, I found myself looking out at a room full of men who were asking me about a decision that needed to be made. One of them said: "How do you want to handle this?"

I paused to think. Then suddenly a light went on. I sat up straight, lifted my chin, and said, "Well, I'm a lady, and I'm going to handle it like a lady."

Where did that *voice come from?* I wondered.

I'd never said those words out loud before. (Men in that room told me they'd never heard anyone say them before, either!) But in my voice that day, I heard all the women I knew growing up in the South—women for whom being a southern lady was a source of confidence and strength in times of trial and a source of joy in good times.

On that day, I especially heard the voice of my grandmother Dorothea.

Dorothea was smart, ambitious, and brave. She had a degree in education from Tennessee Tech and a master's from Peabody College at Vanderbilt University, one of the first such degrees ever earned there by a woman. A firm believer in women's rights and civil rights, Dorothea had a brilliant academic mind and she dreamed of traveling the world. But because of the times, she found her choices limited and ended up becoming a first-grade teacher at a local school. She never did get to see the world as she'd hoped.

Still, she maintained exquisite poise throughout her life, opposed injustice wherever she found it, and commanded everyone's esteem and attention—especially mine. She was at once tough and beautiful. She could make you feel infinitely welcome but also let you know when you'd pushed her too far. She was impeccably mannered, but she loved to see a whole mess of neighbors, their kids, and random pets tearing across the lawn. To me, she was the epitome of southern womanhood.

Dorothea always said that it was a combination of beauty and strength that made southern women "whiskey in a teacup." We may be delicate and ornamental on the outside, she said, but inside we're strong and fiery. Our famous hospitality isn't martyrdom; it's modeling. True southern women treat everyone the way we want to be treated: with grace and respect—no matter where they come from or how different from you they may be. Dorothea taught me to never abide cruelty or injustice. The Golden Rule, she said, applies to everyone.

My mother, too, taught me this by example. I visited her when she was teaching at Tennessee State University (known best, perhaps, as the place where Oprah got her journalism degree in 1986), and there I got to know the powerful black women with whom she worked. They did not tolerate disrespect or discrimination, and they organized to make

Dorothea and Charlotte

Dec. 1937

Dot and Geo. W. 1937

Dot and Mary Butler Monticello 1936

1936

Mother and Dad in Virginia 1935

sure they were heard. They taught me that things only get better for everyone when all voices are at the table.

Back then as a young woman, and now as a mother and female entrepreneur, I've taken to heart their call to change the story by changing the storytellers. I think about that so often as I grow my companies, try to teach my children to hold good values, and as I strive to tell the untold stories in work I produce.

To me, southern womanhood is about both the teacup and the whiskey—the music and the manners, the hospitality and the fight for fairness. Some people think that caring about "silly" things like cooking or fashion is mutually exclusive with "serious" politics. But my mother and grandmother and their friends taught me that finding pleasure at home—whether in a family dinner or a book club or a backyard barbecue—can give us the strength to go out into the world and do incredible things.

This book is intended as a tribute to the diverse group of awe-inspiring southern women who I grew up admiring. These were women who always looked elegant and put-together and were quick with a warm smile, but who were also the undisputed bosses at their places of business and in their homes. For them, southern hospitality meant extending a hand to everyone—whether a party guest who seemed left out or someone in the community who needed help or a young person at work who needed mentoring.

When I was a little girl in pigtails and Coke-bottle glasses, listening to Dolly Parton cassette tapes and watching *90210* and *Designing Women*, I imagined that when I one day left the South, I would see the world and do important things. When I told a teacher that I aspired to be the first woman president, she said, "I'll be the first one to vote for you, Reesey!"

ABOVE, LEFT TO RIGHT My grand-mother Dorothea loved seeing me and my brother, John, dressed up. My grandfather Jimmy approved of overalls.

Well, I didn't become president (nor, alas, did I achieve another early goal: marrying Willie Nelson), but I did become president of a production company that makes movies and TV shows with strong female characters. And I have traveled all around the world, to places I never dreamed I'd go. In a lot of ways, I'm living out my grandmother's dreams. She couldn't do so many of the things I get to do, so I don't take these opportunities for granted for one second. And I do everything I can to make sure those opportunities and more are there for my daughter and for other young women.

Still, now that I've seen the world, you know where I'm happiest?

In the South. In Nashville. Surrounded by friends. Listening to country music. A glass of sweet tea in one hand and a barbecue sandwich in the other. I've learned to appreciate so much about my childhood—from the lessons I learned about treating people fairly to the way I was taught to tend a garden and bake a casserole. Back when I was younger, I fought to lose my accent. But today I'm so proud of where I'm from.

Unfortunately, I have to be in other places an awful lot of the time. But luckily, over the years I've found ways to conjure up the South's spirit wherever I happen to be. I take the South everywhere I go, with bluegrass, big holiday parties, and plenty of Dorothea's fried chicken.

It's become sort of an obsession of mine, spreading the gospel of southern living. My southern heritage informs my whole life—how I value generosity, how I decorate my house, and how I make holidays special for my kids—not to mention how I talk, dance, and do my hair (in these pages, you will learn my fail-proof, only slightly insane hot-roller technique).

I'll share Dorothea's most delicious recipes, and you'll hear about my favorite southern traditions, from midnight barn parties to backyard bridal showers, from magical Christmas mornings to rollicking honky-tonks.

That said, if you are looking for a how-to, self-help bible . . . this ain't it. I love a good party, but I don't have a ton of free time, so when it comes to shortcuts and good-enough-ing, I have been there and store-bought that.

What I can promise is that you'll see how I keep my home, how I entertain, and just how much fried food I eat. And you'll see how easy it is for you to bring a little bit of the South home, no matter where you live. After all, there's a southern side of everywhere in the world, right?

I hope you are sitting somewhere comfy so you can curl up and enjoy this book!

Reese

CHAPTER 1

The Magic of Sweet Tea

One thing about life in the South: people drop by. And it's the law of the land that if someone shows up at your door, you have to offer them something to eat or drink. At the very least, you have to serve them a glass of ice-cold sweet tea.

Every day, before my grandmother Dorothea did just about anything else, she would fill a big jar with tea bags and fresh water and set it on the back porch in the sunshine. The tea would sit there all day brewing. When the sun had done its job, Dorothea would take the jar inside, stir in some sugar and ice, and set it out for us in a pitcher. She called it sun tea, and we drank it with every meal. It is the world's best pairing with country-fried steak and collard greens.

When I moved to California, I was homesick, so I started having friends over for dinner, trying to bring the spirit of those back-porch meals to Hollywood. And in preparation for those meals, I would always make my grandma's sweet tea. Sweet tea reminds me of the South . . . with a capital *S*. It takes me back to those days spent running barefoot around the backyard, catching lightning bugs with my hands. It reminds me of leisurely meals with family and friends, listening to chatter about the neighborhood. I was delighted to learn during my early days in California that, with the right food and company, it can be just as much fun gossiping in a Hollywood living room as it was on a screened-in porch back home.

summer on the porch

If I give you a recipe, you know
you're a friend of mine. And no recipes
are closer to my heart than my grandmother's
tea recipes. Here they are, plus some
snacks to go with them!

Dorothea's Sun Tea & Tea Punch

Pecan-Crusted Chicken Skewers

Vegetable Plate-in-a-Jar

Frozen Fruit Salad

Dorothea's Sun Tea

8 black teabags,
such as orange
pekoe

1 gallon water

**FOR THE SIMPLE
SYRUP**
1 cup sugar

1 cup water

1. Place the teabags in a gallon-sized Mason jar and fill with water, letting the tags hang over the lip of the jar. Top with the lid and screw on the ring. Set the jar in a sunny spot outdoors. Let brew for 4 hours.

2. While the tea brews, prepare the simple syrup: Bring the sugar and water to a boil in a small saucepan, stirring until the sugar has dissolved. Remove from the heat and let cool. The syrup may be stored in the refrigerator, tightly sealed, for up to 1 month. Serve syrup on the side so guests can sweeten their tea to taste.

Dorothea's Tea Punch

Sun Tea

Lemonade

Orange juice

Cinnamon

Sprig of mint

Vodka (optional)

Sun Tea is as easy as it gets. And it's a great base for making other refreshing drinks. My grandmother's Tea Punch is always a big hit, especially when it's hot outside and you can barely eat anything, which is a lot of days in the South. For Christmas, I'll often give friends Mason jars with a delicious brand of tea and my tea punch recipe inside.

1. Mix equal parts Sun Tea, lemonade, and orange juice.

2. Throw in a dash of cinnamon and a sprig of mint.

3. Serve over a lot of ice.

OPTIONAL (unless I've had a really long day—in which case, mandatory): Spike with vodka.

Pecan-Crusted Chicken Skewers

8 chicken tenders

Kosher salt

Freshly ground black pepper

½ cup mayonnaise

2 tablespoons grainy Dijon mustard

½ cup finely chopped pecans

½ cup panko bread crumbs

¼ cup finely grated Parmesan cheese

This is a nice light snack for a summer night. Kids *love* these.

1. Rinse the chicken and pat it dry. Season with salt and pepper. Arrange a rack on a baking sheet and set aside.

2. Stir together the mayonnaise and mustard in a wide, shallow bowl. Combine the pecans, bread crumbs, and Parmesan in a separate wide, shallow bowl.

3. Coat the chicken in the mayo mixture and then roll in the crumb mixture to thoroughly coat. When all the tenders are breaded, place them on the rack and put the whole pan in the refrigerator for 1 hour.

4. Preheat the oven to 400°F. Bake the chicken on the rack over the pan in the preheated oven for 15 to 20 minutes. Serve immediately, at room temperature, or chilled (though they won't be as crispy). Skewer for easy eating.

Vegetable Plate-in-a-Jar

FOR THE VINAIGRETTE

1 small shallot, minced

Pinch of kosher salt

Freshly ground
black pepper

3 tablespoons red
wine vinegar

⅓ cup olive oil

1 tablespoon chopped
fresh basil

FOR THE SALAD

2 cups shredded
romaine hearts

1 cup diced yellow
bell pepper

1 cup halved
cherry tomatoes

1 cup cooked peas
(English, lady,
pink-eyed, or
crowder)

1 cup diced celery

½ cup sliced scallions

½ cup feta cheese,
crumbled

There's nothing quite as cheerful as a bunch of freshly picked farm-stand vegetables marinated in a Mason jar.

1. Combine the shallot, salt, pepper, and vinegar in a small jar. Set aside for 10 minutes to allow the shallots to soften and flavor the vinegar. Add the oil and basil. Place the lid on the jar and shake vigorously to emulsify the dressing. Set aside.

2. Prepare the layered salads by dividing the ingredients evenly among 4 pint-sized jars. Place ½ cup lettuce in each jar and top with the bell peppers, tomatoes, peas, celery, scallions, and feta. Drizzle 2 tablespoons of the vinaigrette over ingredients in each jar. Top with a tight-fitting lid and gently turn each jar over a few times to distribute the dressing without displacing the layers. Refrigerate up to 2 hours before serving.

Frozen Fruit Salad

1 pint fresh
strawberries, diced

6 ounces (¾ cup)
sweetened
condensed milk

1 medium can
pineapple tidbits

2 bananas, chopped

2 cups whipped topping,
plus extra for serving

Sprig of fresh mint

The ladies at the Picnic Cafe in Nashville serve this. It might sound weird, but I promise it's the most delicious simple dessert you've ever tasted—and wonderfully refreshing on a hot day.

1. Combine the strawberries and milk in a blender and puree until smooth.

2. Remove the pitcher from the blender and stir in the pineapple, bananas, and whipped topping (do not blend).

3. Pour the mixture into ten 4-ounce jars and freeze overnight. To serve, top with a dollop of whipped topping and a mint leaf.

CHAPTER 2

Wicker & Wallpaper

I grew up in a neighborhood full of beautiful old Nashville homes with big white-brick facades and generous wraparound porches. There were sweeping lawns and manicured hedges, columned verandas made inviting with big white rocking chairs. Honeysuckle and kudzu crept up lampposts.

We spent a lot of time on those porches, which often featured swings we could sit in for hours. Some also had daybeds, which I always found so quintessentially southern: during the day guests could nap on them, and at night kids could camp out and sleep in the cool night air. That's what I picture when I think about southern homes: lots of porches—and of course ceiling fans everywhere. It's hot, y'all.

I was born close to the Garden District in New Orleans, so I have always had an affinity for that area. I could walk around for hours and look at the gardens. I love Charleston, too, where the architecture and the colors are so gorgeous and not like anywhere else in the world. Wavy old glass windows decorate the beautiful candy-colored buildings that sit side by side on the cobblestone streets. Southern charm at its best.

In Nashville, it's not uncommon for a family to live in a home for four generations or more. Many of my friends' homes were their grandparents'. And traditions are maintained. My grandma grew up with peonies, and when she made her own home, she planted her own beds of the glorious perennials. My brother and sister-in-law

live there now, and those peonies are still blooming! It makes me so happy that their children live in a house my grandparents built.

Those old Nashville homes are usually decorated with furniture from several different eras, as well as lots of heirlooms, such as oil paintings of ancestors and antique rugs. And there's nearly always at least some amount of wicker. I can't even tell you how obsessed I am with wicker furniture. I have it in the Draper James stores, and I have it in my house. I love it because it's not only really comfortable but also light and easy to move. That makes it easy to rearrange and accommodate a lot of different configurations.

Now, another thing you'll find in most Nashville homes is a wide array of patterned wallpaper. Let's discuss wallpaper for a minute . . . I love wallpaper. Almost every room in my house is wallpapered. Wallpaper can make a little room, such as a powder room, into a big surprise. My powder room has wallpaper with giant fish on it . . . all these fish, just swimming around without a care in the world. And don't get me started about a bird motif . . .

My mom, whom we now lovingly call Grandma Betty, was an art major in college. She ended up becoming a nurse because it was a more practical profession, but she's an artist by nature, and now that she's mostly retired, she's a watercolor painter. She loves to play with color and appreciates beautifully designed things.

I rely on her for advice whenever I need to decorate an interior. She helps me pick out fabric for furniture and drapery, and she's really drilled it into me that it's important to pick out things that are built to last, with classic colors and textures. She's brilliant at finding ways to tie things together.

OPPOSITE Peonies and old family photos decorate my mantel- piece. And on the wall is a beautiful Harry Benson photograph of Dolly Parton given to me by one of my very best friends.

My mom is different from my grandma when it comes to choosing furniture. My grandmother loved antiques; my mom likes more practical things. I think I'm a blend of the two. I like beautiful things that are durable because I have three kids and three dogs. Life is messy. Really, really, really messy. But I like the mess. I think that's a southern thing—recognizing that kids and animals are going to come tromping through spaces and it's important to plan for it.

Whenever I see lifestyle magazines where everything's so clean, I wonder, "Where's all the junk?" The first thing I figure out when furnishing a room is where to put the junk. Two words: secret storage. The key to a harmonious and clutter-free living area, especially when you have kids, is to hide everything. I'm talking about closets everywhere, drawers on everything, and ottomans that

are really storage chests. Baskets for Legos. Shelves for games. Just please don't open any cabinets in my house . . . I'm afraid there might be a waterfall of toys coming at you!

It's important to me that my home feel welcoming. I want people to feel like they can sit on the furniture. You can have a beautiful house, very well decorated, but you have to be able to sit down or else it's not a *home*. I don't want my kids to be scared that they're going to break a chair by looking at it. It's not a museum, for Pete's sake!

I also love surprising details all over the house, from a light fixture here to a pillow there. My best girlfriend is very particular about her house's doorknobs. She says, "Doorknobs and handles are the jewelry of your house." Can you tell she's southern?

An Ode to Quilts

Handmade quilts are a wonderful part of traditional southern decorating. My grandmother collected old quilts, and she had some from her childhood that had been made by her great-great-grandmothers. I have stacks and stacks of them in my home. They remind me of the South and the tradition of people talking and making something together as a collective. They make me think about the women who came before me, who fought for my rights and fought for me to have a better life. I still have my grandmother's old blue-and-white and red-and-white quilts, and sometimes I use them as tablecloths at Christmastime. I even have the quilt that was on my grandmother's bed when she was a little girl, and I treasure it.

Flea Market Strategies

You can get a ton of stuff for the home, cheap, at a good flea market. Plus they're a great way to have a fun-for-the-whole-family day out.

When I was growing up, my mom's kitchen window was always full of little ceramic animal figurines. My mom particularly loved figures that were dressed up in professional outfits. One was dressed up as a fireman. Another was trick-or-treating. My mom got most of her little figurines at flea markets. She always let me pick out something when we went, and now I do the same with my kids. It's really fun to give kids $10 and see what they buy, and whether they buy something immediately or hold their money and weigh the pros and cons of a purchase. I would always spend my allotted money on myself immediately, but my brother, John, would always save it.

Recently I came home from the flea market with a little frog soap dish. I put it on my windowsill. I stood back, admiring the little frog in the window. It was so jaunty, so charming, in the way it caught the sun. I loved its character and its little hat and its . . . *Oh, dear God*, I thought in a flash of horror, *I've become my mother!*

CHAPTER 3

Hot Rollers, Red Lipstick & *Steel Magnolias*

Like a lot of women in the South, I love dressing up. I launched my clothing company, Draper James, because no one else seemed to be making the sorts of affordable, simple, pretty dresses I like to wear day to day. Also, I didn't really see anybody talking much about southern women or appreciating their sense of style.

That said, if you went back to my elementary school class and told them I'd become involved in the fashion world in any way, shape, or form, they'd laugh you out of the room. I discovered fashion late. When I was growing up, my mom was a nurse and had neither the time nor the temperament for fashion. And I think she liked seeing me have the freedom to run wild outside with the boys. That meant that I grew up as a tomboy, wearing

my brother's hand-me-down Izod shirts and tube socks. I was not exactly fashion-forward.

Well, my grandma Dorothea had something to say about that. Day to day, my mother's nonchalance reigned, but twice a year, my grandmother would step in and take me shopping at the fancy, family-owned department stores down on Fourth Avenue in Nashville. We would make a day of it, and she would let me pick out three outfits, including a "Christmas dress" and a "spring dress," often in dainty prints and pastels, with puffed sleeves and smocking. (It would always look great with the orchid or gardenia corsages my dad would get for me, my mom, and my grandmother to wear for Mother's Day and to Easter parties.) We also bought matching saddle shoes or Mary Janes.

Shopping with Dorothea was a thrill. I came away with perfect, elegant new clothes, and the stores were such a pleasure to shop in. In the weeks leading up to Easter, one department store, called McClure's, displayed real live bunny rabbits you could pet. During Christmas, it had a model train and served spiced tea and hot chocolate. But I loved those shopping trips most of all because they meant time learning from Dorothea.

My grandmother looked rather like the great classic film actress Barbara Stanwyck, with a strong nose and blond hair. She worked at looking good, too. She loved *Life* magazine and the *Saturday Evening Post*, *Vogue*, and *Harper's Bazaar*, and she would clip out ads to study the clothes, makeup, and hairstyles. Her favorite thing to do was go out to lunch with her girlfriends and then people-watch at the mall.

There was not a single day of the week when she wasn't beautifully put together from head to toe. She even wore a dress and pearls

to garden in (though she'd pair them with cute little sneakers). Honestly, I don't think I've ever seen a picture of my grandmother when she wasn't wearing something that was the exact right thing.

When she took me with her shopping, she taught me what looked good and what didn't. There on Fourth Avenue with Dorothea is where I learned just about everything I know to this day about flattering silhouettes (you can't go wrong with fit and flare) and colors (for example, if you're blond like me, you should probably have some bright colors in your closet). Dorothea wore only brightly colored printed clothes; she hated solids. If you had a black dress on, she would ask, "Why are you wearing that? Did somebody die?"

Most of all, I learned from Dorothea that fashion trends are overrated. To look good, a dress doesn't necessarily have to be up-to-the-minute fashionable. It just has to make you feel good. And you always feel good, I've found, when you're dressed appropriately for whatever activity you're doing. If you're riding a horse, you want to wear riding boots. If you're at a cocktail party, it's nice to be in a cocktail dress. Dressing for Christmas or Easter was about showing your respect.

Dorothea said that presenting yourself well is a way to show others you care about them. My grandmother did the work of teaching me about clothes and taking me shopping, so she expected me to be dressed appropriately when we went out to see a show. And if you're a little girl going to *The Nutcracker* or the symphony with your grandmother, you'd best put on some white tights and white Mary Janes. To this day, I have the voice of my grandma in my head. If I'm going to the theater and am tempted to wear jeans, there she is, saying "But it's the *theater*." And I change.

Poor Dorothea would not be happy to see how many people travel in athletic wear these days. "You don't wear sweatpants on an airplane," she used to say. "It's a privilege to fly. Make sure you wear a nice outfit." I guess she is why I have a real mental block about wearing workout wear all day long. I just don't do it. I think you gotta get up, you gotta work out, and then you gotta get dressed in a real, proper outfit by ten in the morning.

I would never judge anyone for doing otherwise. But if I did it myself, I just know my grandmother would haunt me with that line she always said: "Only wear sweatpants when you're supposed to be sweating."

ABOVE, LEFT AND RIGHT My grandmother Dorothea with my adoring grandfather Jimmy. In that middle photo, I suspect she was in mourning, because otherwise you almost never saw her in dark clothes.

Crown of Glory

Now for hair. Southern women are famous for big hair. Not for nothing do we like the saying "The higher the hair, the closer to God." That said, I basically know only one way to do my hair: hot rollers. At the end of this chapter, I'll show you how it works.

The hot-roller technique is for every day, but when you need a professional, you head to the hair salon. Every Tuesday my grandmother had a standing appointment to have her hair done at Mr. Ray's in Belle Meade Plaza, and every Thursday she had another appointment to get her nails done. I often went with her to both. Once we got to Mr. Ray's, my grandma would hand me some money and let me walk next door to buy penny candy or a bottle of soda from the deli.

Hair salons are a huge part of the life of the southern woman. They're like a secret club. Most women spend a lot of time there; depending on what they're getting done, sometimes an appointment can last three and a half hours. I learned a lot about women and their ideas about life just by sitting there and listening. Perhaps that's how I learned to be a storyteller, just listening to all of those ladies spinning yarns about their lives. Were they all exactly, 100 percent true? Not necessarily. But my mom has a saying about this: "It doesn't have to be true to be told."

I think a lot of people suspect that all women do at salons is complain about their husbands or gossip. The truth is that they talk about everything. How do they want to change the world? What do they want to do with their lives? What are their big dreams and goals? What are their disappointments in life?

OPPOSITE I just have to show you the impressive hairdo in this portrait that hangs in my friend's home in Nashville. Isn't she beautiful?

I'll tell you what else they talk about an awful lot: politics. And not necessarily national politics, though they do that, too, but things going on in the community. For women, a lot of social activism starts in the field of beauty. Just look at Madam C. J. Walker, the first American woman to become a self-made millionaire, via her innovative hair products. Once she became rich and famous, she gave so much back, including the construction of a YMCA and donations to the NAACP, and she was able to give sales jobs to thousands of African American women.

While we're on the subject, I'm so proud that Nashville played a significant role in the civil rights movement. Fisk University is where Congressman John Lewis, who marched on Selma, Alabama, alongside Martin Luther King Jr., studied. Another famous Fisk student, Diane Nash, organized the nonviolent sit-ins in 1960 that desegregated downtown Nashville's lunch counters. Tennessee's Highlander Folk School, where the song "We Shall Overcome" was written, trained activists—among them, Rosa Parks—and developed a literacy program that helped people become qualified to vote.

And for southern women, so much organizing happened in hair salons. There's a fabulous book, *Beauty Shop Politics: African American Women's Activism in the Beauty Industry* by Tiffany M. Gill, about African American hair salons and their owners during the 1960s— women who changed the entire social landscape of the South. For these women, civil rights activism and community social life went hand in hand. They helped one another plan companies and elect leaders and build empires. Thanks to their bravery and entrepreneurship, this country is a better and more just place. Beauty salons can transform more than your hair.

Put Your Face On

Southern ladies do tend to love their makeup. My mother wasn't that into it, but my grandmother sure was. She taught me so many makeup rules that I remember to this day. For example, she always said that makeup should look natural. If you have freckles, you should still be able to see your freckles a little bit even after you put on foundation and powder.

And like my grandmother before me, I'm obsessed with lipstick. Putting on lipstick makes me feel ready for the day and ready for the world. You've got to learn how to apply it properly, though. When I first started doing it, I kind of looked like Ronald McDonald. It takes practice.

One historical note that I just love: When the suffragettes were marching, at one point they started wearing red lipstick so they would all be wearing the same bold color and stand in solidarity with one another. I love how this little thing many women had in their purses became a powerful political symbol. It's a reminder that we don't have to diminish ourselves as women to be seen as strong. You can push for societal change and you can love getting dressed up. You don't have to choose.

When I was a teenager, I attended a weekend makeup class taught at a local beauty school by a former Miss USA contestant named Sharon Steakley. Makeup lessons are pretty much just a southern thing, I think. I mean, I also did all the normal after-school things—dance, theater, cheerleading, talking on the phone too much—but yes, on top of that, I took a class in lip liner and eyebrows. Some of the lessons have really stayed with me. For example, Ms. Steakley showed us how to curl our eyelashes. "Never do this in the car," she said in a hushed, ominous tone. "If you do, and the car stops short, you might rip all your eyelashes out." Fair warning!

Another of her key lessons was the importance of blending. You don't want to have big streaks of foundation or blush or eyeshadow. And you have to make sure that your face and neck aren't radically different shades.

Ms. Steakley tried to help us understand that a little goes a long way, but I have to say that particular lesson is lost on my mother—particularly where blush is concerned. My mother is a big fan of blush. She'd say, "You don't look awake if you don't have your blush on!"

In second grade, on the way into school for picture day, I heard my mother's voice: "No, no, get back here!" She attacked me with the blush brush while muttering "You just don't look awake." As a result, I have on so much blush in my second-grade picture that I look like I have a sunburn.

These days, I can slap on a full face of makeup in about twenty minutes. That's the short version. Like a good Ms. Steakley pupil, I much prefer the intricate, painstaking, meticulously blended version, but I don't usually have that much time.

How to Hot-Roller Your Hair

One thing every southern woman knows how to do: hot-roller her hair. You learn young, and it's like being invited into a secret society of womanhood when your elders teach you this secret. And you never, ever forget it. To this day, this is the only way I know how to do my hair. I can't blow out my own hair. I can't even straight-iron it. But boy, do I know how to do hot rollers. And now I will pass along this wisdom to you.

You need six giant hot rollers—or seven or eight, depending on how much hair you have—mousse, hair spray, and a fair amount of time.

1

Apply mousse (mousse: it's not just for the '80s!) to every section of your hair.

2

Roll up your hair into the heated rollers and clip them down.

3

Get into the car to go wherever you're going with the rollers in your hair. Pro tip: Roll down the window to let the outside air cool the rollers. The whole drive, pray you do not see any ex-boyfriends or current crushes until your hair is finished.

4

Once you have arrived at your destination, right before you're about to get out of the car, take all the rollers out, turn your head over, brush your hair upside down, and then flip it back. Spray with hair spray. Now use more hair spray. Big hair is traditional, but in this day and age it is fully acceptable to go for shape over height.

With great ceremony, I recently handed down this cherished secret of southern womanhood to my daughter. Her reaction? She thinks I'm nuts and says irons are much easier. To each her own, that's what I say.

Let's Talk About the *Steel Magnolias* Beauty Parlor Scene

I'm all for acting classes and camps, coaches and mentors. But if you don't have access to any of those things and want to study acting, there is good news: you can learn all you really need to know about acting from repeated viewing of the beauty salon scene in *Steel Magnolias*.

Hear me out. The women in this scene are all fascinating, fully drawn characters. The dialogue is fast-paced and complex. So much happens in that eleven-minute scene (yes, I've timed it) that I am always in awe. You realize that scene must have taken three days to shoot—and was worth every second. Those few minutes manage to showcase the beauty of southern female friendships and how important beauty shop politics are—and the scene even advances the plot.

If you need a refresher: Dolly Parton is doing Julia Roberts's hair at the same time that everyone's chattering away about weddings and life and gossip. And then Julia Roberts has a medical emergency. Throughout, there's such incredible character work. You have seven fully formed people with distinct motivations and complex relationships with one another. They stay deeply in character the entire time, sending looks at one another that convey decades of small-town dynamics. In the flash of an eye, you see love and hate and compassion and annoyance and everything in between. If each of those women is an instrument, that scene is a symphony!

Again, take acting classes if you can, but if not, just watch that one *Steel Magnolias* scene over and over. Study it well, and I guarantee you will improve your craft. And even if you don't dream of being an actor, I feel your overall happiness will improve just by reflecting on lines such as Sally Field's comeback to Julia Roberts's declaration that her wedding colors are "blush and bashful": "Her colors are pink and pink."

CHAPTER 4

The Subtle Art of Dinner Parties

Dinner parties are one of my favorite ways to spend an evening. I love everything about them, including the planning, and I pay attention when I go to great parties so that I can improve my own. Once I was at a party with indoor and outdoor seating, and everywhere were these huge trays of minimeals—noodles and vegetables, salads, steak cut super thin. Everything was delicious. And it all felt informal and easy. Everyone was relaxed and happy, flitting around trying all these delicious foods and then lounging, chatting happily with their new friends. I took notes!

Dorothea's Seven Hostess Tips

My grandmother loved throwing dinner parties, and she was amazing at it. When I throw parties, I try to emulate her style. Here are some of the things she did that I try to do, too.

1. Invite people of different ages and backgrounds to make conversation more interesting.

2. Send invites (or save-the-dates) at least two weeks in advance.

3. Do as much in advance as possible (setting the table, prepping the food).

4. Decorate with fresh flowers and unscented candles.

5. Have a fully stocked bar, as well as lots of ice and sweet tea, and both red and white wine for cocktail hour and dinner. Keep everyone's glasses full.

6. Serve dinner about one hour after the start time on the invitation.

7. Put on Louis Prima or Ella Fitzgerald and let the party begin!

Of course, the first step to having your own party is to figure out who to invite. It's key to get a nice, enlivening mix of folks. I always have to fight the temptation to reinvite the same gang who made for the last fun party. I'll think, *That mix worked great, and it was a Friday night . . . I know, I'll have the same people over again on another Friday!*

But you can't have the same party twice. It's never the same. Plus, unexpected surprises are part of the fun of hosting. You can't rehash the same party theme or compare this year's Christmas party to those of years past. You have to think of each new party as an opportunity to make new memories.

I tend to invite people who have something in common or know some of the same people, and I try to have a good mix of single friends and couples. Always invite at least one single friend! It makes conversation more lively. You also need a ringer or two, people who really know how to make things fun. I have a couple of friends who are my go-to guests, great people to keep the party hopping, like my friend Howell. Howell is from Houston and can talk to anybody about anything for at least three hours—and have the best time doing it. I call him my all-purpose guest. He can chat just as delightfully with a five-year-old as an eighty-five-year-old.

Bless his heart, my younger son is like this, too, and has been since he learned to talk. Starting at the crack of dawn, it's all "Mom, I slept all night. Mom, are we in New York? Mom, were you alive when Pluto was a planet? Mom, are you awake? Mom . . ." In twenty years, I will certainly enlist him for all my dinner parties.

When it comes to invites, I check people's availability at least two weeks in advance, because people are really busy nowadays. When I get a time when everybody can come—and I usually go for a Saturday night, because people tend to be too tired on Friday after working all week—then I try to get everyone to confirm.

Now, this is my little public service announcement: If you get invited to something, it's incumbent upon you to RSVP as soon as possible. A quick "no" is better than a long "maybe." People go to a lot of trouble to plan a party, and it's a big deal to open your home. What's more, it's essential to show up if you say you will. I have a busy life, but I still don't cancel unless it's a superduper emergency—I'm talking a hospital-visit, in-the-newspapers-the-next-day emergency. Being tired just isn't a good enough excuse. C'mon! Make an effort!

One trick I use to determine whether or not to say yes to an invite is: Would I want to go right then and there? If the party were that second, would I get dressed and rush out of the house to go to the party? If the answer is yes, I probably do want to go, but if the answer is no, I don't accept the invitation.

Once I know who's coming to dinner, I start to think about food on the Wednesday before a Saturday party. I do shopping and prepping on Friday. I'll get fresh produce, some good bread, almonds, and olives, and I'll prep as much as I can. In my experience, it's particularly nice to prepare a special meal in honor of someone—such as gumbo for a person from New Orleans or catfish for a friend from South Carolina.

A lot of people have moral or religious or health-based dietary restrictions, and a lot of people are just plain picky. That's why I always include at least two dishes that are vegetarian, so no one feels left out and we don't have to make a big deal out of it. They can just skip the meat and have the salad and vegetables, and no one even notices. In addition, I usually send out an email the night before, asking about allergies. That way, when I'm cooking, I can keep the nuts or shellfish or whatever it is separate from everything else if need be.

Early on the day of the party, I'll set the table, with the glasses and everything, because I hate stressing at the last minute about things I can do anytime.

Cooking a big meal is all about the timing. I will look at everything I'm cooking and figure it out like a math problem, what needs to go in the oven when. If you're cooking or roasting chickens or potatoes, you know it will take a while. Start that bird first!

I often buy dessert, because making a cake in addition to a whole dinner is pretty intense, and I feel it doesn't usually add so much. I'll buy a cake, or I'll just make something really simple, with store-bought ingredients, or I'll ask the kids to bake something. Ava makes the best chocolate chip cookies. And who doesn't eat chocolate chip cookies? I don't fully trust a person who will turn down a salty chocolate chip cookie. My grandma had a really good recipe for what she called "Cowboy Cookies," and I'll share that with you in this chapter.

When people arrive, the first thing I do is make sure they have a drink. You have to be mindful if someone doesn't drink alcohol and have soda or seltzer for him or her. I usually have a nonalcoholic option like club soda with fresh-squeezed juice and a fun garnish such as lavender sprigs or fresh mint. A fake cocktail can be delicious and festive, and it's more cheerful than a glass of water or a can of Coke.

For the drinkers, I always have red and white wine available, and a full bar. These days, it seems that the most popular liquors are vodka and tequila, so I make sure we're stocked with those at the very least. I'll add napkins with clever sayings, like "The only thing I throw back on Thursday is a cocktail" or "Wine because kids."

I make sure there's something for people to snack on as soon as they arrive, because I've found most people show up really hungry at the 7 p.m. start time. You don't want them all twitchy waiting for dinner to be served. I always set out cheese and bread, olives, hummus and crudités, or rice crackers—I *love* rice crackers.

At eight, once everyone's had some drinks and snacks and settled in, I announce dinner, and we go sit at the table. I'm very proud of my dinner bell. It's a pretty brass one I found online ages ago. I let the kids ring it when dinner is ready or whenever anyone wants to make a toast. Unfortunately, my five-year-old likes using it to let us know when he wakes up . . . at 5 a.m.

Dinner parties usually follow a predictable arc. As everyone eats and talks and drinks, they get more enthusiastic and louder. Then people start getting tired, and usually the whole thing is wrapped up by 10:30 or 11 p.m.

Ideally, that is. I've found that sometimes it's hard, especially when it's a fun party, to get people to know when to call it a night. Once I invited a couple I didn't know very well over for a brunch party with another eight or so people. We had a lovely time. At around 2 p.m., everyone had gone except that one couple. They wanted to swim. Why not? Sure! So they stayed and swam. Then it was late afternoon, and they asked, "Do you have anything we can eat?"

Bold move, but no problem. I put out snacks.

My husband had to run to the store, and when he came back they were still there.

Snacks turned into dinner.

Dinner turned into after-dinner drinks.

Jim and I were looking at each other like, *What do we do?* They were very nice. But I started to think, *These people are never going to leave. Maybe they just live with us now?*

It had been a really fun day. But we hadn't planned on those last several hours. I had to make dinner out of nothing. Fortunately, I found some chicken and sausages and vegetables in the fridge and roasted all that together the way a girlfriend taught me. You end up with a lot of food, and you can just serve a salad with it.

Cut to 11:30 at night. This is where being a southern lady can be a bit of a burden, because, like some sort of party-throwing robot, I am programmed to keep entertaining until everyone leaves my premises. Yet that couple had been at our house since eleven in the morning. Finally Jim cracked. He stood up and said, "Well, I'm going to bed." Just like that. He walked upstairs and went to sleep. At last the couple left, and I collapsed into bed, too. Even the most hospitable hostess needs sleep.

Dorothea's Seven Guest Tips

1. RSVP promptly. Everyone's time is valuable, and it's no joke to organize a party.

2. When in doubt about how fancy it is, dress up. Better overdressed than underdressed!

3. Bring something. You can't go wrong with a bottle of wine.

4. Introduce yourself to everyone you meet—first and last name, please—even if you think they should know you already. And try to talk to everyone, especially anyone who seems a little lost or left out.

5. Offer to help the hosts carry trays, set out water, clear, or whatever else needs doing. Even if she says no, it's nice to offer.

6. Leave at a reasonable hour. Never be the last person to leave a party. This is hard for southern ladies, because we're taught to shake everyone's hand and wish them a warm goodbye and thank them for the delicious meal and say how fun it was to see them and so on and so forth . . . It's like the opposite of what they call an Irish goodbye or French exit. A proper southern goodbye can take hours.

7. To show you appreciate the hospitality, send a quick, genuine thank-you the next day—by phone, email, or, even better, handwritten note—and offer to reciprocate!

Refresher Cocktail Two Ways

4 ounces limeade
(I like Santa Cruz
Organic or Simply
brand limeade)

2 ounces tequila blanco
(leave the tequila
out for the non-
alcoholic version)

3 dashes Fee Brothers
mint bitters

2 to 4 ounces ginger ale

Sprig of fresh mint

Lime wedges or slices

Tip: To save time, mix up a large batch of this drink in a pitcher minus the tequila, then have the bottle of booze on hand to add to the glasses of only those who would like to imbibe.

I love a good cocktail. But I also have a lot of friends who don't drink, and I hate to see them without something festive in hand during a cocktail hour. When planning a party, I try to always make sure there's a fun, fizzy mocktail in a pretty glass with a garnish for them. Here's a delicious cocktail that's festive with or without the alcohol.

Stir the limeade, the tequila (don't add for the mocktail), and the bitters together in a mixing glass. Pour into a highball or other pretty cocktail glass over plenty of ice. Pour the ginger ale on top for a fizzy top-off and garnish with mint and lime.

NOTE: Fee Brothers bitters has about as much alcohol in it as vanilla flavoring (40%) has. I looked at some AA forums, and some people think it's okay to put bitters in drinks, but others don't. So I think it's more responsible to say don't add bitters for the nonalcoholic version.

Crudités with Garden Green Goddess Dip

GREEN GODDESS DIP

¾ cup Greek yogurt

¾ cup mayonnaise

1 medium garlic
clove, peeled

2 teaspoons anchovy
paste (or 2 to 3
minced anchovies)

1 cup loosely packed
flat-leaf parsley
leaves

¼ cup loosely packed
fresh tarragon leaves

3 tablespoons minced
chives

Finely grated zest and
juice of 1 medium
lemon

½ teaspoon kosher salt,
or more to taste

¼ teaspoon freshly
ground black pepper

Combine whatever vegetables you love on a platter. I use broccoli (just the florets, blanched), radishes, baby carrots, French green beans, and endive leaves. Blanching certain vegetables for a few minutes in boiling salted water followed by plunging them into ice water will help lock in their bright color to make them prettier on the platter, too.

TO MAKE THE DIP

Process all the dip ingredients in a blender until smooth. Keep chilled until ready to serve. Store up to 1 week in the refrigerator.

southern dinner party

For dinner parties, I like to have a main dish with fish or meat and then hearty vegetarian sides so everyone can find something they like. And biscuits—always biscuits!

Cheddar Biscuits

Shrimp and Grits

Sautéed Baby Kale

Mud Pie Trifle

Cowboy Cookies

Cheddar Biscuits

2 cups all-purpose flour plus more for rolling

2¼ teaspoons baking powder

¾ teaspoon baking soda

½ teaspoon salt

6 tablespoons (¾ stick) butter, chilled and cut into small cubes

¾ cup sharp cheddar cheese, shredded

1 cup buttermilk

¼ cup butter, melted

Flecks of sharp cheddar cheese add flavor and color to these biscuits. I like to make them smaller, using a 1½-inch biscuit cutter or small juice glass to cut them out. For a party, these are fantastic filled with ham, fig jam, or my favorite, tomato jam. (For biscuit-making advice, see "Biscuit-Making Tips" on page 259.)

1. Preheat the oven to 425°F.

2. In a large mixing bowl, sift together the flour, baking powder, baking soda, and salt. Cut the cold butter into the flour using a pastry cutter until the texture resembles coarse oats or small peas. Fold in the cheddar cheese and pour in the buttermilk, mixing with your hands until just incorporated. The dough will begin to come together, but do not knead so much that it becomes a ball. Turn the loose dough out onto a floured surface and, with floured hands and rolling pin, bring the dough together and begin to roll it out. You may have to add some sprinkles of flour to the dough, your hands, and the pin if it sticks. The key to tender biscuits is not to work the dough too much.

3. Roll the dough out to ½ inch thick, fold the dough over onto itself once, and roll out again to ½ inch thick. Turn the dough over again in half and then again into fourths—this creates flaky layers. Roll out one last time to ½ inch thick.

Continued…

Tip: I put a snake of dough on the outer edges to prevent spreading.

4. With a biscuit cutter dipped in flour, cut out biscuits by pressing straight down and back up—don't twist the cutter—cutting them out as close to each other as possible. Place the biscuits on an ungreased baking sheet right up against the edges of the sheet and line them up with the edges of the dough touching each other. Gently gather the dough scraps from the first rolling into a mass, working the dough as little as possible, and roll out and cut out more biscuits. Use the scraps from the second batch to roll into a "snake" shape. Press the shape against any biscuits that may have a bare edge where the biscuits have not filled the tray.

5. Bake for 15 to 20 minutes, rotating the pan 180 degrees halfway through, until golden brown. Remove from oven and immediately brush with melted butter.

Shrimp and Grits

FOR THE GRITS

1½ cup grits (not quick-cooking—I like stone-ground)

1 teaspoon salt

4 tablespoons (½ stick) butter

FOR THE SHRIMP

2 tablespoons olive oil

1 tablespoon butter

1 medium onion, chopped

1 small green pepper, chopped

3 cloves garlic, minced

1 (14 oz.) can diced tomatoes with liquid

1 teaspoon Cajun seasoning (I like Tony Chachere's Creole Seasoning)

2 tablespoons tomato paste

2 pounds medium-large raw shrimp, peeled

½ cup water

2 teaspoons Worcestershire sauce

Salt to taste

Chopped fresh green onions for garnish

The combination of creamy grits with slightly spicy, tomatoey shrimp is a classic coastal dish in the South. It's comforting and hearty, but in an elegant serving bowl it can also be a perfect meal to serve at a dinner party.

TO MAKE THE GRITS

In a medium saucepan, bring 3 cups of water to a boil over high heat and stir in the grits and salt. Bring back to a boil, stirring occasionally, then reduce the heat to low, stir in the butter, and simmer for about 15 minutes. The grits will absorb all the water, so you will need to stir them occasionally, and you can add more water if they become too thick. The grits are easy to keep warm on very low heat, just adding water when needed, but you must stir them every now and then to keep them from sticking to the bottom or clumping.

TO MAKE THE SHRIMP

In a large skillet or sauté pan, combine the olive oil and butter over medium-high heat until the butter is melted. Add the onion and green pepper and sauté until they begin to soften, about 4 minutes. Add the garlic and cook for 1 more minute. Stir in the tomatoes and their liquid, the Cajun seasoning, and the tomato paste. Cook for 2 to 3 minutes and add the shrimp, stirring for about 2 minutes, until the shrimp turn pink. Add the water and Worcestershire sauce and cook for another 2 to 3 minutes until heated through but not boiling. Taste for seasoning, and add salt if needed. Serve immediately over the warm grits and garnish with chopped green onions.

Sautéed Baby Kale

2 tablespoons olive oil or vegetable oil

3 cloves garlic, minced

2 (9 oz.) packages pre-washed baby kale

Salt and pepper to taste

Lemon juice or vinegar to sprinkle on top

Hearty greens are such a good side dish—healthy and easy to make quickly. There are so many wonderful greens available in the market washed and ready to use. You can buy packages of organic baby kale to keep in the fridge. Or plant some! I always have kale in my garden because it's so easy to grow. This recipe calls for two 9-ounce packages of baby kale. It seems like a lot, but when you start to sauté the kale it will wilt down significantly. No matter what, a good rule of thumb is to figure on a big handful of greens for each serving. After sautéing, a little squeeze of lemon juice or a sprinkle of a fancy vinegar, such as balsamic or a fruit or champagne vinegar, is a great way to finish off the dish and add a bit of acidity.

In a large sauté pan, heat the oil over medium-high heat. Throw in the garlic and stir for 1 minute, being careful to not let the garlic turn brown. Toss in the baby kale in batches, allowing the first few handfuls to wilt a little so that you have room to add the rest of it. Sauté the kale and garlic together until the kale is just wilted and still bright green. Season with salt and pepper to taste. Squeeze a little lemon juice over the greens or have some lemon wedges or a fancy vinegar available on the table for guests to sprinkle on top.

Mud Pie Trifle

1 (8 oz.) container of Cool Whip

1 (5.9 oz.) box of instant dark chocolate or fudge pudding

3 cups coarsely crumbled chocolate cake (you can make a quick chocolate cake from a mix)

2 cups crushed Oreo cookies

Mississippi Mud Pie is a church cookbook favorite, typically layered with (gourmet purists, stop reading now!) chocolate pudding, Oreo cookies, and Cool Whip. It's a guilty pleasure of semihomemade decadence. Layering the ingredients in a fancy trifle dish is the ultimate "high-low" hack.

This recipe always makes me think of Miss Betty, who ran a little Nashville restaurant in Sylvan Park. When I was a little girl, my parents worked late on Thursdays, so my grandparents would take me and my brother there at five o'clock for dinner. Oh, we loved it there.

"Miss Betty," we'd say when we arrived, "what pies do you have today?"

And Miss Betty would list some eight or nine pies that she'd made that day, from lemon meringue (my grandmother's favorite) to Mississippi mud (my favorite). And every pie would have a mile-high meringue on top.

After my grandmother died, I took my kids to eat at Miss Betty's. I'd been holding it together okay until then, but Miss Betty came up and gave me a big hug and I instantly burst into tears.

"I am so sorry for your loss," she said to me. "Every Thursday I think about you and your grandparents."

Miss Betty has passed away now, too. She fed her community and made so many people happy. I think about her often—especially when I see a cheerful dessert.

Defrost the Cool Whip according to the directions on the container. Make the instant chocolate pudding according to the directions on the box. In a trifle dish or deep-sided bowl, create a 1-inch layer of cake crumbles on the bottom of the dish. Top with about an inch of the pudding, and then top that with a layer of crumbled Oreo cookies. Spread out a layer of the Cool Whip. Repeat the layering process, using all the ingredients, and top with a layer of Cool Whip. Decorate the top if you like with more cake crumbles or Oreos or a combination of both. Serve immediately, or keep chilled until about 1 hour before serving.

Cowboy Cookies

3 cups all-purpose flour

1 tablespoon baking powder

1 tablespoon baking soda

1 tablespoon ground cinnamon

1 teaspoon salt

1½ cups light brown sugar

1½ cups granulated sugar

1 tablespoon vanilla extract

1½ cups softened butter

3 eggs

2 cups old-fashioned rolled oats

2 cups Rice Krispies cereal

2 cups shredded coconut

1½ cups chopped pecans

1½ cups semisweet chocolate chips

Some people prefer these with chocolate or no coconut or extra nuts or whatever, and, as in the Wild West, there are no strict rules. It's easy to omit or change up ingredients, because this basic dough is very forgiving. One other tip: I find that once you have the cookie dough in the pan, if you put the pan in the freezer for 15 minutes before baking, the cookies won't come out too flat.

1. Preheat the oven to 350°F.

2. In a large mixing bowl, sift together the flour, baking powder, baking soda, cinnamon, and salt. In a separate mixing bowl, cream together the brown sugar, granulated sugar, vanilla extract, and butter with a mixer until light and fluffy. Add the eggs, one at a time, to the butter mixture and mix well before adding the next egg. In batches, add the flour mixture to the butter mixture and mix until just combined. With a spatula or wooden spoon, fold in the oats, Rice Krispies, coconut, pecans, and chocolate chips.

3. Using a spoon or a small scoop, drop spoonfuls of dough onto a cookie sheet about 1½ inches apart. Place the cookie sheet in the freezer for about 15 minutes. Take directly from the freezer to the oven and bake for 10 to 12 minutes until golden brown. Bake them slightly less if you like chewier cookies, longer if you like them crispy.

Table Settings

Tip: If you don't know which side the bread plate or drinks go on (or which bread plate or water glass is yours when you're seated at the table), make the okay sign with each of your hands. Your left hand will make a lowercase *b* for *bread*. Your right hand will make a lowercase *d* for *drink*. I taught my kids this and they use it all the time.

Nowadays, no one expects to see a perfect table setting at a regular old dinner party, but I think it's helpful to know the old-school rules, if for no other reason than if you find yourself at a formal meal, you're not undone by a cake fork. For those who are curious, here are the traditional southern ways to set a table: you use the acronym FORKS, where the dinner plate is the O:

Fork, O for plate, Knife, Spoon.

Yes, I know that spells FOKS. Just go with it.

Seating

The guest of honor is traditionally seated to the host's right and is served first. Try to mix up seating so couples aren't always together. They already see each other every day! And you want to give them something to talk about on the way home.

Serving

A buffet is considered a bit more casual. For a seated meal served at the table, plates are served from a guest's left side and taken away from their right. Serving moves counterclockwise, with the host served last. For family-style service, platters are passed from left to right. Each guest should hold the platter for the guest on his or her right.

Casual

Salad Plate
Service Plate

Water

Wine

Salad Fork

Dinner Knife

Soup Spoon

Entrée Fork

Teaspoon

Formal

Bread Plate

Place Card

Red Wine

Butter Knife

Dessert Spoon

Water

White Wine

Cake Fork

Teacup

Salad Fork

Saucer

Entrée Fork

Soup Cup
Saucer
Salad Plate
Service Plate
Charger

Dinner Knife

Soup Spoon

Teaspoon

CHAPTER 5

If It's Not Moving, Monogram It

Southern ladies have a reputation for loving all sorts of embroidery, and I'm here to tell you that this reputation is 100 percent based in fact. Even my brother, John, knows how to needlepoint. It's something my mother taught both of us at a very young age. Towels, bedding, bags, cocktail napkins, dog collars—nothing is finished without at least a couple of initials in colorful stitching. If there's a wedding or a new baby on the way, don't stand between a southern woman and a monogram store; you'll get knocked down. We have a saying in my family: If it's not moving, monogram it.

My love of monograms started early. When I was a little girl, my best friend, Ashley, had white towels with pink embroidery that matched the wallpaper in her bathroom. The towels also

matched her pink floral coverlet and her pink floral pillows. Everything was piped in the exact same light pink. To me, that was the *ultimate* southern-lady décor. The chicest thing ever. I ran home and told my mother I wanted monograms, too, so then every year she gave me a monogrammed towel or monogrammed beach bag.

I think a monogram says to people, "Hello, there. I'm southern." Or maybe it says, "Don't steal my stuff." All I know is I hardly ever see monograms in New York or LA, but I can walk into almost any nice house in Nashville and there will be monogrammed sheets on the bed. It's just how we grew up. You take really good care of them, and you keep them forever. One of the very first things I bought after I had my daughter, Ava, was monogrammed pillow shams for her bed.

I can spend hours in a monogram shop with my mother—and have. We love to discuss which colors and fonts and styles are our favorites. To the untrained eye, all monograms look the same, but once you've spent some time around them, you start to see the variations. Some are formal, while others are more contemporary.

RTJ

reese witherspoon

REESE & JIM
· EST. 2011 ·

reese witherspoon

Beckett Andrew Bray
Oct. 15, 2017 8:47pm
7lbs 2oz 21inches

At this point, if you are not from the South, you may be thinking, "Uh, monograms come in different levels of formality and different styles?"

I'm so glad you asked. Why, yes! There are many subtleties, even when it comes to which letters you choose to embroider. Traditionally, your married-name initial goes in the middle, with your maiden initials on either side. So, for instance, I have a typical long southern name: Laura Jeanne Reese Witherspoon. I married someone with a last name starting with a T. So my current, more modern monogram is, reading from left to right: R with a large T and a W. A more classic monogram would be L, T, J. There are also nuances of font. A curlicue script is traditional and formal. Some wild and crazy young upstart monogrammers use bold, modern fonts. Fascinating, right? Well, to me it is! I know . . . I'm weird.

My grandmother had monogrammed silver and china, some of which I inherited. My mother has her mother's silverware, and though it doesn't have the Witherspoon monogram, it's a nice family heirloom with her maiden name on it. I'm also obsessed with stationery because I write a lot of thank-you notes. Do you doubt my obsession? I have formal stationery *and* informal stationery. Yes, there is a *big* difference. The formal is on sturdier stock, and the monogram is in a more traditional font.

The monogram's gift potential is limitless.

For a baby, I think it's nice to do a monogrammed blanket with the date of birth on it. Alternately, you could do a traditional silver cup or spoon, a frame, or a rattle. You get the idea.

For a wedding or housewarming, the list is even longer: towels, sheets, plates, barware, a cashmere or cotton throw, desk accessories,

pretty wastebaskets, frames . . . you name it. A chic wedding gift would be four linen cocktail napkins with a beautiful monogram detail.

One of my favorite possessions, and favorite gifts to give, is a monogrammed keepsake binder. I've kept monogrammed birthday binders for Ava, Deacon, and Tennessee since they were born. Every year on each of their birthdays, I sit down and write a letter from my heart. They grow up so fast, and this is an easy and meaningful way to mark the passage of time. On their eighteenth birthdays, they will get their binders and can look back at all the personal messages I have written to them. It's nice for us all to have this remembrance of their childhood.

You could do this for a bridal shower, too. All the guests could write a letter to the bride and groom. Then the bride and groom could write letters to each other on their anniversaries. How special will that book be on a fiftieth wedding anniversary? With a monogrammed cover, of course!

Monogrammed Scrapbooks

I love preserving family memories. I keep my favorite recollections and photographs in a special monogrammed scrapbook. In this, as in so many things, my grandmother led the way. Sadly, she died about a year after my oldest, Ava, was born, but that just makes me all the more grateful for the memoirs and photographs and records I have

June and Dorothea.

masters group
X = Jimmy and Dorothea.

Jimmy

Dorothea and Jimmy
Standing Stone - July 21-1940

Steve, June,
Dot and
Jimmy
Standing Stone
July 21-1940

Dorothea
1940

of her. For example, I was so glad she got to hold baby Ava before she passed. I'll never forget what she said, smiling down at her: "That baby's just sweet as sugar." I wanted to make sure we recorded that moment with a photo and detailed caption so that Ava would know she'd had that all-too-brief connection with her great-grandmother.

Dorothea loved keeping records like I do. When I got into movies, she kept scrapbooks with every newspaper clipping about me. She had scrapbooks going all the way back to her own childhood, and we would spend hours sitting on the floor going through them. She had beautiful penmanship and on the back of each photo wrote everyone's name and the date. We don't always think to include dates and full names on our photos, because of course *we* know who the people are and roughly when each picture was taken. But decades from now, our family members will come across the photos and be baffled unless we've taken a few seconds to annotate them.

To this day, I'm grateful for Dorothea's detailed scrapbooks. Thanks to her, I know so much about our family tree and can identify everyone in the old photos. This year, I took it to the next level and had all of it digitally archived. And I try to keep it up, because I want my grandchildren, should I be lucky enough to have some, to remember me and Dorothea and my grandfather Jimmy and my parents, and all the rest of our family who came before them.

OPPOSITE Here are a couple of pages from our family scrapbook. I feel so fortunate that my grandmother kept these careful records.

Nonmonogrammed Gift Ideas (If You *Must*)

I always love to give hostesses those little cheese knives and butter knives—the little ones that are specifically for hors d'oeuvres. Who doesn't need those? Yet I feel like nobody ever thinks to buy them for themselves.

For young women, I vote pearls. They say diamonds are a girl's best friend, but my grandmother Dorothea always said that pearls are a *southern* girl's best friend. A string of pearls is symbolic, a token typically given to mark a rite of passage—confirmation, sixteenth birthday, graduation, or engagement. At church on Sunday, you can glance from pew to pew, and all around you'll see women wearing their best pearls.

One tradition in my family was to give Add-A-Pearl necklaces, whether tiny natural seed pearls on a delicate chain or starter strands of cultured pearls. Those were special-occasion gifts it seemed every girl I knew growing up got. I got mine for my confirmation. Pearls are a particularly great gift for a niece or goddaughter.

For my wedding, a dear friend gave me a pair of engraved brass horseshoes with my wedding date on them that I thought were so clever and that I treasure. When I need to give a wedding present, I'm not usually that creative. In fact, I always give the same thing: a cake plate. Always, always. Because you know what? Cake plates remind you of fun times and good things. No one is depressed when they see a cake plate. A cake is happiness. With frosting on top.

CHAPTER 6

Bluegrass Forever

Being from Nashville, I grew up surrounded by music. The entertainment at our school functions wouldn't be some random garage band but rather famous country singers such as Brooks & Dunn, Amy Grant, or Emmylou Harris. It was normal for me to be around a lot of country music singers. The country music scene was like our Hollywood. And I had so many favorites: Dolly Parton, of course. Alabama. The Oak Ridge Boys were huge when I was little. Rosanne Cash. Loretta Lynn. Barbara Mandrell was a major star, because she and her sisters had a variety show on television. Every Saturday night, we were glued to it. Louise was the funniest Mandrell—she was my favorite, and not just because once at a music awards show she took the stage in hot rollers.

One of the great disappointments of my life was when I didn't get to play Barbara Mandrell in the fourth-grade play. I was gutted. Fortunately, I got to play "Mother" Maybelle Carter instead, complete with autoharp. So I got an early country music history lesson on the Carter Family. Maybe that's why I scored the part of June Carter Cash in *Walk the Line*: my intimate knowledge of all the Carter Family's greatest hits. I knew the lyrics to "Wildwood Flower" before I ever shot one frame of the movie.

My childhood was full of music, and I'm doing the same for my children. There's always music playing, and we're always singing songs to one another. My little boy is named Tennessee, so we sing him the University of Tennessee cheer: *T-E*-double *N-E*-double *S*-double *E*-TENNESSEE! That's how he learned to spell his name. We also sing the University of Tennessee's unofficial fight song, the Osborne Brothers' 1967 country hit "Rocky Top," to him. He thinks it's hysterical. You know how much I like the song "Rocky Top"? I played it at my wedding, never mind that it has a line about "corn from a jar." It reminds me of where I'm from.

To me, bluegrass music is so soothing and comforting. I find it relaxing and just so *happy*, and I'll keep it on in the background as I go about my day. It's got its roots in Appalachia, and it makes me feel like I'm home. I love what Steve Martin said: "The banjo is such a happy instrument. You can't play a sad song on the banjo. It always comes out so cheerful."

Honky-tonkers Don't Cry

My mom, a retired nurse, works these days as a hostess at a honky-tonk.

"Your mom still works after she retired?" someone asked me recently.

I burst out laughing. She doesn't have to; she *loves* to. I beg her to relax, but she insists on working.

"I'm an extrovert," she says. "You can't keep me at home!"

The best way to describe my mother is sunshine in human form: smiling, laughing, always dancing while practicing the deepest gratitude for life. Deeply social and a true optimist, she managed to end every day I was little with something nice to say about her job, and telling me and my brother she loved us. She would sit on our beds and listen to our dreams, frustrations, and heartbreaks and say, "Everything is going to work out. You'll see." I remember crying one night when I was fourteen years old because I wasn't even filling out my training bra. My mom soothed me by saying that my boobs would grow: "In fact, one day they will be so big, you will have to cart them around in wheelbarrows." Did I mention she's funny?

We would watch *Saturday Night Live* together and laugh at the Church Lady and the Cheerleaders. Betty's laugh was always the loudest, just so full and easy. She's not afraid of a good knee slap, either. And boy does my mother love to dance and sing! There is not a day of my childhood when I don't remember her dancing and singing.

A born artist, she never met a blooming flower, dog, horse, landscape, or new city that she didn't marvel at. She finds beauty in simple things: flowers on her front porch, a squirrel in the yard, a visit with her elderly neighbor. One time when I was eleven years old, she heard me and my friend gossiping about a boy at school and she told us we should never speak ugly about people who weren't present. I've never forgotten those words, and I've taught my children that we should always find the best in people like Grandma Betty does.

She found purpose in her work as a nurse and a teacher and she told me long stories about her students, who were trying to become part of the medical workforce in Nashville. She had endless patience to listen to her students and answer their questions, and she took their struggles to heart. She felt pride in her work because she knew those men and women would be serving our community. To this day, I have people who come and tell me that my mother was their teacher, and it fills me with pride.

It always made my day when she came home and told me she had spoken about me in her early childhood pediatrics class. I remember thinking she carried me with her even when she was working. That meant the world to me and showed me the value of being a working woman. She taught me that it was important to tell children how fulfilling work can be so they will want to find that sense of purpose in their own lives. I credit my mother for my work ethic. I am always happiest when I am working because I learned from her that if you love your job and take pride in it, it really doesn't feel like working at all.

That certainly is how she feels now about working at a honky-tonk. For those of you who don't know what a honky-tonk is: it's a great southern nightclub with live music and dancing. *Fun* dancing, too, the kind anyone can do. When I was a kid, I took clogging lessons and learned cotillion dancing, and they were both *work*. But at a honky-tonk, there's no pressure. People of all ages just get up and start dancing, beer in hand. The spirit of the place is such that everybody will dance with anybody. No judgment if you're not a great dancer or need help learning the steps. It's all just in the spirit of fun.

Of course, there's always a show-off or two to keep things lively—that guy who knows every dance, twirls every girl. To me, there's nothing more charming or appealing than a guy who knows how to dance like that. A king of Texas swing? Forget it. He's the only guy you want to dance with. My dear friend, Howell, whom I've men-

tioned as my go-to dinner party guest, grew up in Texas, and he's been dancing like that forever. Naturally, if there will be any dancing at all, I insist that he come to the party with me. And invariably, he's the most popular man in the room. (Maybe Howell's mom should be writing this book instead of me! She knows how to raise a good southerner!)

Full Moon Midnight BBQ Barn Party

My parents instilled a love of music in me early on. We would go listen to live music two or three nights a week, whether it was a bluegrass concert at the park or an evening at the Bluebird Café, where local songwriters test out their newest tunes. Sometimes when there was a full moon during harvesttime, we'd go to a midnight barn party at our friends' big backyard barn. That was my favorite outing.

You'd show up in the backyard while it was still light out, and you'd see a barbecue going and a ton of hay bales set up in a big semicircle around the entrance to the barn. You'd hear crickets chirping, and you'd have to wear cowboy boots because this was a barn, after all, and you never knew what you might step in.

As it got dark, the musicians would appear in the doorway of the barn and start playing bluegrass music. All different kinds of local musicians would join in. It would always start out with one act, then turn into a giant jam band by the end. And we kids were thrilled that we got to stay up until midnight!

You had people from the whole community talking and laughing and the children dancing up a storm on the grass. I think those nights are where my love of music and especially live music began. Bluegrass has been carried down as a tradition from generation to generation, and I love to see it continue. I have a cousin who makes all those old-fashioned instruments such as mandolins and zithers, and I consider it a great tribute to our heritage.

Now, as you might imagine, everyone worked up quite an appetite dancing. As happens so often in the South, at those midnight

barn parties, music and food would go hand in hand. On the buffet table, there was always barbecue. You'd have hamburger buns and different kinds of sauces for different tastes, and then corn on the cob and lots of booze.

These days, the spirit of those barn concerts lives on in some of the parties I go to around Nashville. For example, after the Country Music Awards, Ronnie Dunn and his wife, Janine, used to host a long-standing party where all the musicians would go back to his house and sing around a piano. It was magical. You'd see George Strait, members of Rascal Flatts, Martina McBride, Keith Urban, just singing away together.

The country music community is so inclusive. Its members really care about one another, and there's no divisiveness. There's just this incredible spirit of collaboration in that we are all artists and we all support one another. Those moments of togetherness around a Nash-ville piano are something we can all learn from.

Southern Party Playlist

When I was appearing as June Carter Cash in the film *Walk the Line*, I learned so much about the history of American music, how the Carter Family traced the origins of country to old English folk songs and made sure to record every song for posterity. It made me appreciate the music all the more. Also, my party playlists got a million times better. These days I usually just put "Patsy Cline" into Spotify and let the magic unfold. But if you want to curate your own southern playlist, here are a few songs to get things off to a solid start:

"WALKIN' AFTER MIDNIGHT" PATSY CLINE	**"I LIE WHEN I DRINK"** DALE WATSON	**"LAST CALL"** LEE ANN WOMACK
"WINE, WOMEN AND SONG" LORETTA LYNN	**"SHAKE SUGAREE"** ELIZABETH COTTEN	**"THE DARK END OF THE STREET"** JAMES CARR
"KISS AN ANGEL GOOD MORNIN'" CHARLEY PRIDE	**"JOLENE"** DOLLY PARTON	**"MISSISSIPPI GIRL"** FAITH HILL
"TROUBADOUR" GEORGE STRAIT	**"ORANGE BLOSSOM SPECIAL"** DOLLY PARTON	**"BLOWN AWAY"** CARRIE UNDERWOOD
"BIG RIVER" THE SECRET SISTERS	**"THE TRUTH"** JASON ALDEAN	**"DON'T BLINK"** KENNY CHESNEY
"FAMILY TRADITION" HANK WILLIAMS JR.	**"COMING HOME"** LEON BRIDGES	**"WHITE LIAR"** MIRANDA LAMBERT
"SHADOW ON THE WALL" RUBY AMANFU	**"AMERICAN HONEY"** LADY ANTEBELLUM	**"YOU SEND ME"** SAM COOKE
"BLESSED" MARTINA McBRIDE	**"BOONDOCKS"** LITTLE BIG TOWN	**"CHICKEN FRIED"** ZAC BROWN BAND
"ONLY IN MY MIND" REBA McENTIRE	**"GEORGIA ON MY MIND"** RAY CHARLES	**"TENNESSEE WHISKEY"** CHRIS STAPLETON
"AMERICAN WOMAN" MUDDY MAGNOLIAS	**"BLUE EYES CRYING IN THE RAIN"** WILLIE NELSON	**"MY MIND'S GOT A MIND OF ITS OWN"** JIMMY DALE GILMORE

Brother John's Ribs

FOR THE DRY RUB

¼ cup packed brown sugar

4 tablespoons chili powder

1 tablespoon salt

2 tablespoons garlic powder

2 tablespoons onion powder

2 tablespoons cumin

1 tablespoon cinnamon

2 tablespoons ground oregano

1 teaspoon cayenne pepper

1 tablespoon unsweetened cocoa powder

FOR THE RIBS

4 to 6 baby back rib racks

½ cup yellow mustard

Optional: John's BBQ Sauce (recipe follows)

As you probably know, there's a big argument about Texas barbecue versus North Carolina barbecue versus Tennessee barbecue, and now there's a whole Georgia sweet and smoky . . . Some places do a vinegar-based sauce. Others like to use honey. Of course, I think Tennessee's traditional red barbecue sauce is the best and my brother John's is the best of all. Here's his secret sauce recipe and his famous (in our house, at least!) ribs recipe, too.

TO MAKE THE DRY RUB

Place all ingredients into a jar with a tight-fitting lid or a zip-lock bag and shake until mixed well. Use immediately or keep sealed and stored in a dry, dark place for up to 6 months or until it loses its nice, strong smell.

TO MAKE THE RIBS

1. Remove the thin membrane from the back of each rack if it has not already been removed by the store. Let the ribs rest at room temperature for 30 minutes. Prepare your smoker or grill and bring the temperature up to 210° to 225°F.

2. While the smoker or grill is getting hot, coat each rack of ribs with a few tablespoons of yellow mustard so that there is a thin layer on the front and back of each set (this will help create a brown crust and help a dry rub of your choice adhere; you will not taste the mustard after the meat is cooked). Season the ribs with the prepared

Continued...

dry rub both front and back (preferably a thicker coat on the top, curved side).

3. Place the ribs, curved side up, cupped side down, in the smoker or grill. Cook for 3 hours at 210° to 225°F. Add smoke to the ribs only for the first hour, using wood chips or pellets of your choice (hickory, mesquite, apple chips, or whatever).

4. After 3 hours, remove the ribs quickly and wrap with aluminum foil. Turn the foil-wrapped ribs over, so the cupped side is up, and replace them in the grill or smoker.

5. Cook the ribs for an additional 1 to 1½ hours at 210° to 225° F. The internal temperature should reach 165°F.

Tip: For meat that falls off the bone, don't rush or use high heat. John's mantra: "Slow and low."

OPTIONAL: For wet, sticky ribs, baste the ribs generously with a wet BBQ sauce before wrapping them in the aluminum foil and placing them back into the smoker or grill, cupped side up. Then, during the last 10 minutes of the 4-hour cook time, remove the ribs from the foil and baste them one more time with the BBQ sauce. Place them back into the smoker or grill without the foil, directly on the rack, and allow the sauce to caramelize. Transfer the ribs to a cutting board and allow to rest for 10 to 20 minutes before serving. Another serving option is to cut all the meat off the bones, chop the meat, and serve it on top of a nice salad or on buns as BBQ sandwiches. Serve with corn on the cob, boiled for just a few minutes, and extra sauce on the side.

John's BBQ Sauce

¾ cup (1½ sticks) butter, divided

¼ cup chopped onion

1 clove garlic, minced

1 teaspoon salt

1 teaspoon freshly ground black pepper

1 cup diced tomatoes (fresh or canned)

4 tablespoons ketchup

5 tablespoons apple cider vinegar

2 tablespoons Worcestershire sauce

1½ cups water

3 bay leaves

½ lemon, sliced

1. In a medium saucepot over medium-high heat, melt 4 tablespoons of the butter.

2. Stir in the chopped onion and sauté for 1 minute.

3. Add the garlic and the salt and pepper and sauté for another minute.

4. Stir in the tomatoes and ketchup, then add the vinegar, Worcestershire sauce, water, bay leaves, and lemon slices. Bring to a boil, then reduce the heat to low. Simmer for 15 minutes, stirring frequently.

5. Remove from heat and strain the liquid into a bowl. Stir in the remaining butter, allowing it to melt completely in the hot liquid. The sauce can be served warm or kept covered in the refrigerator for up to 1 month.

CHAPTER 7

The Family Table

These days, I feel as though I can barely sit still for ten minutes without getting antsy. A lot of friends my age have the same issue: we're always looking at our watches halfway through a play or staring impatiently at the clock when we're waiting in line at the bank.

What's going on with us? I used to be able to wait, or to make it through a whole movie without wanting to check my phone or run around the block. For a while, I thought I was just getting older and battier, but now I think it's due to some combination of our faster pace of life, the onslaught of technology, and the feeling that there's so much to do that there's no time to waste.

Family dinner is my only salvation from this affliction. We put all the devices away. I put some hot food on the table. We say grace. It's really important to me for us to appreciate that we have very blessed lives and should be grateful every second of the day for all of our blessings. Grace is a time to raise the kids' awareness that we must take care of others who are not as fortunate and to remind them to think of the big picture.

For as long as we're at the table, the rest of the world melts away. My kids love it when I make simple one-pot meals such as chili or Crock-Pot pot roast. Or noodles with ground turkey and vegetables. Sometimes I'll go all out and do fried chicken and sides.

After saying grace, as we eat, we'll each talk about our day's highlights. It's our little five-year-old, Tennessee's, favorite thing to do. Some people I know call this dinner game "Roses and Thorns": you have to say the best thing (the rose) of your day and the worst thing (the thorn). It's a good way to get out of the "How was school?" "Fine" rut.

Also over dinner, we might play a guessing game where one of us thinks of an animal and the others have to ask questions about where it lives. It's a really good game with little kids. And they get excited because it feels very grown-up and sophisticated to be playing a game with people of all ages. Each person can ask only one question about the animal to try to figure it out. My middle child thinks of things that are so hard that nobody can guess them. But it's really sweet to see the five-year-old trying to figure it out, so serious: "Is it . . . an elephant? Is it . . . a kitten?"

Deacon: "Close. It's a North American marmot."

When Jim and the kids and I are sitting there eating and laughing, I often flash back to family meals with my grandparents, which we'd often eat out on the screened-in porch, complete with soundtrack of the screen door's spring stretching followed by the whapping sound the door made as it slammed. Adults would sip drinks on the porch before dinner and watch the sun go down as the kids played outside,

filling jars with fireflies. I like to think my kids will look back on our dinners this way, how we talked and laughed together over plates of good, filling food—but even more fulfilling conversation.

My grandparents loved our stories, hanging on every word and detail. We felt appreciated and important, as though our opinions mattered. My mother laughed loudest at all my jokes—so I always blame her for making me become an actor. She egged me on, which made me feel even bolder. Her laugh gave me courage. She has the best laugh in the world.

ABOVE   That's me with my mom and grandparents. I've always loved family dinners.

Southern Conversation Starters

Now, heaven forbid anyone spills salt during a family dinner. You have to throw it over your left shoulder *immediately*, or . . .

Well, you know, most of us growing up in the South never quite knew *what* would happen if we didn't abide by the superstition, but we knew it was *bad*.

Here are a few of the more common superstitions we were raised with. I suppose adherence to such arbitrary rules might make us seem a little unhinged sometimes, but when you're constantly on the lookout for omens of ill fortune, it does keep the day lively!

• A hat on a bed is bad luck.

• If you sweep a broom under a young woman's feet, she'll never marry.

• Never stir any liquid with a knife—it leads to strife.

• Walking under a ladder is bad luck.

• If a black cat crosses your path, you'll have bad luck unless you go home and start your trip again.

• A broken mirror means seven years' bad luck.

• Don't put your purse on the floor. If you do, it's "money out the door."

Reese's Corn Bread Chili Pie

2 tablespoons olive oil

1 medium onion, chopped

2 cloves garlic, minced

1 pound ground beef

1 pound ground pork

2 (1.75 oz.) packets chili seasoning

1 (14 oz.) can diced tomatoes

2 tablespoons tomato paste

2 cups chicken broth

2 (8.5 oz.) boxes Jiffy Corn Muffin Mix

2 eggs

⅔ cup milk

1 cup frozen corn, divided

1 cup shredded cheddar cheese

1 (16 oz.) can kidney beans, drained

Optional toppings: Fresh salsa, fresh chopped green onion, sour cream, shredded cheddar cheese

For a weekday dinner with family, you need something that will please both kids and adults and that isn't too complicated to make. My favorite thing is chili pie. This is an easy one-dish dinner if you are using a cast-iron or other oven-safe skillet. If using a baking dish or casserole, cook the filling on the stove top in a skillet or sauté pan and transfer to the baking dish before adding the corn bread batter topping.

1. Preheat the oven to 375°F.

2. In a 9- or 10-inch cast-iron skillet or sauté pan, heat the olive oil over medium-high heat until it shimmers. Add the onion and sauté for 1 minute before adding the garlic. Sauté for another minute and add the ground beef and pork, breaking up the meat with a wooden spoon and stirring until the meat is brown.

3. Drain off any excess fat and stir in the chili seasoning, diced tomatoes, and tomato paste. Mix over medium heat for 1 minute, then pour in the chicken broth. Reduce the heat to low and simmer for 5 minutes, stirring occasionally.

4. While the meat simmers, make the corn bread mixture: Stir together the Jiffy mix, eggs, and milk in a mixing bowl until just combined (do not overmix). Stir ½ cup of the frozen corn and the cheese into the corn bread batter and set aside. Stir the remaining ½ cup of corn and the kidney beans into the meat mixture.

5. If using a baking or casserole dish, transfer the meat mixture from the stove top to the baking dish. Pour the corn bread batter over the meat mixture and bake in the oven for 35 to 40 minutes, until golden brown on top. Remove from the oven and allow to sit for 10 minutes before serving with optional toppings such as salsa, green onion, sour cream, and shredded cheese.

Dolly Parton, Southern Icon

No discussion of the South is complete without a tribute to that eternal symbol of southern womanhood: Dolly Parton.

Here's my Dolly story:

I have a vivid memory of being six years old and skipping rope on the blacktop in my first-grade PE class. My teacher, Mrs. Wright, who is still a teacher at my old school, asked me, "Reesey, what do you want to be when you grow up?" As I've mentioned, by that point I had considered becoming the first female president of the United States or (and?) Mrs. Willie Nelson. But now, at the ripe age of six, I had a new, loftier ambition. Without missing a skip, I said, "Mrs. Wright, when I grow up, I am going to be Dolly Parton."

I was, in fact, convinced that I was going to be her—or at least a funny, smart, blond country music singer in her image. I could see it so clearly: I would have a variety show just like Dolly Parton, I would have her glittery wardrobe, and, above all else, I would have that *voice*.

Well, it wasn't meant to be. I took singing lessons, to no avail. It's one of the great tragedies of my life that I was born without the talent to become a country music singer. In retrospect, it's pretty funny how bad I was at singing—and how long it took for me to take the hint. When I was thirteen years old, I began entering Nashville acting and singing competitions. I'd always win the acting ones, but I would never even place in the singing ones. Still, I continued to sing out! If nothing else, at that stage competing taught me that I always had a song in my heart and that I really enjoyed performing, no matter what sort of feedback I was getting on the vocal part.

Then I got an opportunity to go to camp in the Catskills of upstate New York with hundreds of kids who all had dreams of being on Broadway. I was soon told the following: "You . . . in the front . . . Yes, you . . . Please stop singing. Acting is your thing; focus on that."

Finally I accepted reality. In the long run, that experience taught me that learning what I wasn't good at was just as important as learning what I was. That is a *huge* life lesson.

And that brings us back to Dolly. Because it was there, in the Catskills at age thirteen, that I had to surrender my dream of being her. But sometimes dreams have a strange way of coming true even after you abandon them. At fourteen, I started acting professionally, and then, many years later, I got one of the most important roles of my career: *Walk the Line*. That meant I had to do a lot of research about June Carter and the Carter Family.

Well, my father was a surgeon in Nashville who worked on people's vocal chords. He never told me who his patients were, because he was a professional. But when some of his patients heard that I would be playing Johnny Cash's wife, they offered to send me videotapes and pictures and memorabilia. One of those generous people was Dolly.

That's right, Dolly Parton—*the* Dolly Parton—reached out and offered to meet me and help me to prepare for my role. She said she'd help me with any guidance she could about context for the Carter Family. Well, I was over the moon. And we set a date.

She picked me up in her car. One of her cousins was driving us. And we went to a three-hour dinner. She told me stories from her life in country music and so many things she knew about the Carter Family and especially Johnny Cash. She was incredibly generous with her time and her experiences, which really helped inform my performance. More even than the great insights she had, she gave me *courage*. Leaving that dinner, I felt emboldened to play the role, even though I still feared I wouldn't be credible as a country music singer. In fact, when the film's director, Jim Mangold, had hired me, my response had been, "Great! You're going to get LeAnn Rimes to sing for me, right?" I had, after all, been hearing, for about twenty years, people saying "Please don't sing."

What would Dolly do?

But, Jim felt confident I could sing on screen, and Dolly told me I could do it, so I had to have faith. I took singing lessons for seven months to prepare. Our producer, T Bone Burnett, coached me, too. He taught me that singing isn't about perfection; it's about emotion.

He guided my performance so that even if mine wasn't the most proficient voice possible, it always came from my heart.

Still, I confess I thought I was going to throw up every single time I shot a scene where I sang. (Have you seen the movie? There's a lot of singing, y'all!) But I just drank a beer and did it anyway. And it all worked out okay. A lot of key moments in life are like that: You can be nervous as all get out. Just drink a beer and do it anyway.

June Carter Cash ended up being a very important role in my career. And I've always been really appreciative of everyone who contributed in any way to that film—especially Dolly Parton—for helping me get there.

Dolly and I have stayed in touch since, and she's remained a very caring and supportive figure in my life. When I started Draper James, she was one of the first people to say, "Hey, how can I help you?" She even came down and shopped! And when I called her and asked, "Can I create a product that says 'What would Dolly do?' Because I think it all the time," she said, "Absolutely!"

She continues to inspire me to no end. Here is a woman who came from profoundly humble beginnings, yet she has thrived and continues to be so deeply grateful to and appreciative of every person who has helped her, including every single fan. I love her positivity and her cultural outreach in the South. Did you know that as part of her far-reaching literacy program, Imagination Library, she sends free books to children ages birth to five in communities all around the country— and in the U.K., Canada, and Australia? "Who knows," she's said of her work, "maybe there is a little girl whose dream it is to be a writer and singer. The seeds of these dreams are often found in books and the seeds you help plant in your community can grow across the world."

Beyond being a fabulous entertainer, she's a wonderful person. So for me, she's the ultimate southern icon.

Honorary Southern Icon
HRH the Duchess of Cambridge

Why do southern women like British royalty? I have a girlfriend whose entire Instagram account is made up of photos of the royal family. As a little girl, I used to watch everything that came on television about Princess Diana. My mother follows the rise and fall of the royals' fortunes closely. Why? I asked her this the other day, and we decided that southern women like how the royals value family and how they're always doing good for others. There's also their keen attention to propriety and sense of tradition. Plus, of course, the dresses! Southern women love pomp and circumstance.

Still, I felt relatively immune from the obsession with the royals until a few years ago when I was invited to meet Kate Middleton. She had just married Prince William, and she was coming to Los Angeles for a fund raiser. I don't even know how I got so lucky as to receive the invitation. The *scream* that issued from my lips upon receiving it—you would have thought I was going to die. I wake up early, mind you, but on that day I was up at 4 a.m. doing my hair. That's early, even for me.

"I've never seen you this excited," my husband said.

He wasn't kidding. I was up, dressed, and waiting by the door by 7 a.m. Jim took pictures of me in the car. You can see rays of happiness shooting out of my face. I love Kate Middleton *that* much.

And she did not disappoint! She was just lovely and warm, elegant and composed. She also told a joke, and I immediately fell under her spell. She's just as magnificent as she seems to be. She's a very compassionate, socially conscious, deeply caring person.

What's more, it takes a very special person to decide to commit to that kind of life, to choose to be under public scrutiny every moment. Now that she's in that position, her entire life is in service, *forever*. I am so in awe of that kind of dedication.

CHAPTER 9

My Grandfather's Garden

I know I've talked in this book an awful lot about my grand-mother Dorothea. I do associate flowers and beautiful scents with her. She had about a dozen bottles of floral perfumes, some with cut-crystal stoppers. Her favorite scent was Joy. As a little girl, I loved to sneak in her room and dab a bit behind my ears.

Yet her husband, James Witherspoon, my grandfather Jimmy, is who I think of when I think of southern flowers. He was one of the greatest influences in my life. I worshipped him. I followed him everywhere as a child and would drop anything to play checkers with him on the porch. The tallest person in our family (a whopping six foot one . . . we are a family of shorties!), he was a World War II veteran—he'd served as a fighter pilot—and a high

school principal. He'd grown up on a farm in Midlothian, Texas, and he kept farmers' hours, waking up each morning at dawn. My grandfather was never happier than when he was working around his magnolia trees, hydrangeas, peonies, and irises, which are both the Tennessee state flower and my mother's favorites.

When I stayed with my grandparents, from the age of three, I'd wake up early, too, so I could have the honor of helping my grandfather in the garden. We would eat Cheerios and bananas before heading out to work: mowing the lawn or painting the house. He always worked in white coveralls, coming in only for a sandwich at midday and then again around five o'clock to shower and change for dinner. Being his helper was my very first job. As I followed him everywhere, I asked a million questions about the garden, the gutters, the lawn mower, the cars. You name it, if he was working on something, I had a question, and he always had a patient answer for me.

His flower garden was his pride and joy, and he did every bit of the work on it himself. In the huge expanse of my grandparents' backyard, my grandfather nurtured, planted, and maintained a prolific garden. He dug up the entire backyard each spring—the tired beds full of dried-out, gone-to-seed plants left from the end of the previous growing season—and would spend hour upon hour turning the soil and planning out every single thing he wished to grow for the season ahead.

From the nursery catalogs that filled my grandparents' mailbox, he would select the seeds to plant—tomatoes, okra, green beans, and lots of flowers, too. He grew masses of zinnias for the rabbits to eat so

they'd leave his vegetables alone. Each day he would walk his garden and water and check on his plants, wandering from row to row.

To this day, one of my most vivid memories is being in the garden with him, probably around the age of five, following behind him with my endless chatter. He stopped and said, "Reese, less talking, more working on the plants." I learned to stop and appreciate the plants.

Because I was paying so much attention that summer, I noticed exactly when the tomatoes turned red, and it was a thrilling day for me. At harvesttime, I walked the rows with him, picking mountains of beans, and then I'd sit on the back porch with my grandma, snapping and stringing them for hours. In the mornings, Jimmy and I would deliver fresh tomatoes to neighbors' doorsteps.

Jimmy showed me firsthand what a life of hard work and service looks like. His garden reflected his nurturing spirit. For the rest of my life, the scent of fresh tomatoes will bring my mind racing back to those times.

Today, at my house in California, I plant roses and vegetables in a small garden. It brings me such joy, especially in the early summer when I see the first signs of growth. My kids aren't much for gardening so far, but one day I think they'll remember that I love flowers, the same way I remember so clearly how my grandfather Jimmy did.

Honeysuckle

Honeysuckle grows like wildfire in the South. It covers the hedges, creek sides, and garden walls. It grows wherever there is water and heat—so basically the entire South—from May to October. That sweet floral fragrance reminds me of my youth. We had a big honeysuckle bush in our side yard that would blossom every spring. My brother taught me to pinch off the blossom and pull the stem to suck out the nectar. The neighborhood kids and I could spend hours doing that. As if they weren't pretty enough on their own, they often attract hummingbirds and butter-flies, too.

CHAPTER 10

Making Special Occasions Special

Special-occasion entertaining is some of the best entertaining there is, because you have an event around which all the activities arrange themselves. In this chapter, I'll talk about the usual special events, like weddings and baby showers, but I'll also mention a few South-specific ones, like the Kentucky Derby, Steeplechase, and the Nashville Symphony Ball. What they all have in common is a sense of community—and, of course, great food.

Weddings

I happen to love a church wedding, because I'm a practicing Episcopalian—not to be confused with a pescatarian. My daughter, Ava, went through a period for two or three years where she didn't eat meat, only fish—a pescatarian diet. At that time my son Deacon was in kindergarten, and they were talking about vegetarians. "Does anybody know anyone who has a different diet?" the teacher asked. Deacon raised his hand and said, "I do! My sister is Episcopalian. She eats only fish."

Growing up, I loved church. I was in the choir for nine years. I loved going every Wednesday after school and every Saturday to practice. I loved singing loud up there at the front every Sunday. We were told that if you weren't singing loudly, God couldn't hear you. Choir was great practice for being in theater. I learned how to project to the back pews. And you have to be on time and church-ready by the first church service! All those little old ladies are waiting.

I had such a positive, accepting religious upbringing. Our church was traditional but progressive at the same time. The parish and ministry were both diverse. We learned that Christianity is about making people feel welcome and reserving judgment of them. The church for me has always been a safe place to learn about doing work for others, being respectful, and being part of a community. In Nashville, you'd go to church on Sunday, and then you'd see the same folks on Monday at work or school or the grocery store. Small-town living has its upsides.

So, naturally, I love a church wedding. But I also think it's nice if festivities take place outside. It's so great to enjoy the beauty of being in nature at this important moment in your life, letting nature set the

ABOVE How beautiful was my mother on her wedding day?

mood. Even a little rain can be so beautiful (and I like the superstition that it's good luck!).

At southern weddings, there are always a lot of bridesmaids. Let me tell you why I think that is: people are so darn polite in the South, and they don't want to hurt anybody's feelings.

But it's also because you want the maximum number of people standing around you, helping you make this huge commitment. The people you invite to your wedding are the people who are supposed to guard your vows of marriage and help you enjoy the good times and make it through the bad times. You know, there are ups and downs in everybody's marriage. No one can escape that. And beware of anyone who goes on and on about their "perfect" marriage. It's usually not the full truth. The friends you invite to your wedding are supposed to be there for you both, so you need to be very thoughtful about how you pick them.

A piece of advice: Do not let anyone pressure you into having random people at your wedding. It's such an intensely personal and private moment, you know? And those are the people you're going to be telling your hopes and dreams to; it's not about getting another blender or letting some great-aunt show you off. It's about real vulnerability, and you are the ones who get to choose who gets to see that vulnerability. But, most importantly, it's a party!

When it comes to the food, I always love it when there's both a groom's cake and a bride's cake. Usually, the bride's is a traditional white cake and the groom's is a chocolate cake. Both are important, because variety is the spice of life.

And of course *the* most important thing at any wedding is the music. People must dance—early and often, and with the maximum number of people on the dance floor. At my wedding, my husband's friends very sweetly danced with all the older ladies. My mom had the time of her life, and so did my husband's mom. Always find a cute, game friend who will make it his job to keep all the old ladies happy by dancing with them. You get a lot of points in my book for being the guy who dances with grannies.

I've seen a trend toward kid-free weddings, and I have to say, it's not ideal in my book. I think going to weddings is an important way to show children what marriage means, what community means, and what commitment is all about. If they don't get to see the ritual enacted, how are they going to learn? Children need to understand that people stand up for each other, that they care for each other, that they care for their families, and that when they're in love they want to bring their families together in celebration. I also feel that having kids around keeps us mindful of what a wedding is about: it's a family occasion, not a fashion show.

And now let's get real: I've had two weddings. The first time I got married, it was at a gorgeous old farm property in Charleston with giant moss-covered oak trees. Charleston is one of the most magical places in our country; it's no wonder so many people get married there. The second time, I got married at my own house, which was a beautiful working farm, with chickens, dogs, and goats running around. (Yes, I had a farm for a while, before I realized how hard it is to have a farm. I sold it to people who wanted to be full-time farmers. I miss the chickens, but it's better for everyone this way.)

So there I was in one of the rooms of my farmhouse getting dressed, and my best friend since college, Heather, grabbed my hands. I braced for a pep talk.

"Are you ready?" she asked.

"Yes," I said, taking a deep breath.

"Are you excited?" she said.

"Yes," I said and smiled.

"Good," she said, "because you only get married for the second time once."

I burst out laughing. But my eyes teared up, too. Because it was true! Life isn't about perfection. There is no rule book. Life has many different chapters, and every chapter deserves celebrating.

That point was driven home again moments later, when I went to stand up and leave the room to head to the ceremony. I'd been sitting on a bed in my dress for some time, with my bridesmaids and flower girls and other close family members around me. We were all talking away. Then, when the time came, I began to stand up . . . and found I was rooted to the bed by my veil. I looked back and saw several little children sitting on my veil, eating crackers. Crumbs everywhere! Heather and I cracked up. Let's face it, folks—life is not a perfect tableau. So just brush off the crumbs and get the show on the road.

And you know what? That wedding day was one of the most beautiful, joyful days of my life, but of all the glorious moments— from my future husband, Jim, standing there with our pastor waiting for me to the sight of so many people I love dancing together—for pure joy, it's hard to beat the memory of Heather making me laugh out loud or that image of those precious little boys and girls sitting on my veil, happily snacking away in a field of white tulle.

Baby Showers

Baby showers are just so fun—especially, I think, for those of us who have been mothers for a while. We get to share stories from the trenches, and we get to marvel at how impossibly small and precious baby socks are. Heather made a homemade cake for my last baby shower, and it was gorgeous: three layers of white cake layered with whipped cream, with fresh flowers on the top.

Not everyone loves shower games, but I can't get enough of them. I especially like games that involve all the generations. I'm partial to guessing people's pregnancy cravings, and I love a big gender reveal, like when you cut the cake and the icing inside is either pink or blue. Whoever invented that is a *genius*.

One of the things we did for a girlfriend of mine was that each of us had to bring a piece of fabric for the baby that meant something to us. We told the story of what it meant, and then all the pieces of fabric were sewed into a quilt for the baby. Now her daughter has this gorgeous keepsake filled with love forever. How special!

pre-gaming a gala

This menu is straight-up from my mom.
My parents went to a lot of cultural events in
Nashville, especially for the Nashville Symphony,
and when they did they would have friends over
first for drinks. It was win-win for me. They'd
serve tasty hors d'oeuvres, and I'd get to admire
the ladies' dresses. I always longed to go out with
them, but I was too young, so my brother, John, and
I would stay home playing Boggle and eating all
the leftover snacks. Now, I get dressed up and go to
fancy parties, too, but I always make sure we have
these snacks before we go!

Confetti Betty's Champagne and Ginger Ale Cocktail

Smoked Pecans

Crab Puffs

Confetti Betty's Champagne and Ginger Ale Cocktail

1 (750 ml) bottle Champagne or Prosecco

24 ounces chilled ginger ale

Candied ginger for garnish (optional)

My mom has become known as "Confetti Betty" by my friends and family because she figured out how to use the animated confetti effect when she sends text messages. Ah, Technolady! If anyone needs a tech-savvy grandma, I have one. Look out, Silicon Valley!

Combine the Champagne or Prosecco and the ginger ale in a punch bowl or large pitcher. Stir lightly to combine. Ladle or pour into champagne glasses and drop in a piece of candied ginger, if desired, to serve.

Smoked Pecans

4 cups pecan halves

¼ cup liquid smoke
BBQ sauce

¼ cup water

1 teaspoon salt

1 teaspoon smoked
Spanish paprika

These pecans get their smoky flavor from both a splash of liquid smoke and a dash of Spanish paprika.

1. Preheat the oven to 300°F.

2. Place the pecan halves in a large bowl. Whisk together the liquid smoke, water, salt, and smoked paprika and pour over the pecans. Let sit for 1 hour to allow the pecans to soak up the liquid.

3. Drain the nuts of any excess liquid. Spread in a single layer on a parchment-lined baking sheet. Bake for 20 minutes, until dried out and toasted.

Crab Puffs

6 ounces crab claw meat

½ cup water

½ cup milk

¼ pound (1 stick) butter

3 tablespoons Dijon mustard

1 teaspoon salt

⅛ teaspoon cayenne pepper

1 cup all-purpose flour

4 eggs

2 cups (8 ounces) shredded Gruyère cheese

2 tablespoons minced chives

These retro bites are downright addictive and are always the first thing to go at any party. They can be made ahead and refrigerated or frozen and reheated. Plus it's fun to say, "Would you like a crab puff?"

1. Preheat the oven to 400°F.

2. Line a baking sheet with parchment paper.

3. Pick over the crab meat, removing any bits of cartilage or shell.

4. In a medium saucepan, bring the water, milk, butter, Dijon mustard, salt, and cayenne pepper to a boil over high heat. With a wooden spoon, stir in the flour until a dough forms. Reduce the heat to low and continue to beat with the wooden spoon until the dough pulls away from the sides of the pan. Remove the pan from the heat and set aside for 2 minutes.

5. Beat in the eggs one at a time until incorporated after each addition. Stir in the cheese, crab meat, and chives. Drop rounded tablespoons of dough about 2 inches apart on the prepared baking sheet. Bake for 20 to 25 minutes, until puffy and golden brown. Let cool on a wire rack for a few minutes before serving, or cool completely and refrigerate to serve later. (Reheat at 350°F for 8 to 10 minutes.)

Kentucky Derby

Dad used to drive us to Louisville, Kentucky, to see the Kentucky Derby when we were kids. It was so close to Nashville. Just a three-hour drive. He would give us money to bet on one horse, so we were very invested for the two hours it took for the race to begin.

Now I have Derby parties at my home, because who doesn't want to get dressed up, drink mint juleps, eat Derby Pie, and wear a fun, giant hat?

Here are some of my favorite Derby party recipes, courtesy of my friend Annie Campbell.

kentucky derby party

The main thing at a Derby party is the classic drink: a mint julep in a silver cup. This can be supplemented with some snacks like deviled eggs and hot brown bites. Don't forget a Derby Pie to eat once the race is over so everyone can celebrate their betting victories or recover from their favorite horse's defeat!

Mint Juleps

Paprika-Dusted Deviled Eggs

Kentucky Hot Brown Bites

Chocolate Derby Pecan Pie

Mint Juleps

From the kitchen of Annie Campbell

FOR THE SIMPLE SYRUP

1 cup sugar

1 cup distilled water

FOR THE MINT JULEP

2 bunches fresh spearmint

4 cups bourbon

Powdered sugar for garnish

TO MAKE THE SIMPLE SYRUP

Mix the sugar and water in a small saucepan. Heat to dissolve the sugar. Stir constantly so the sugar does not burn. Set aside to cool.

TO MAKE THE MINT EXTRACT

Wash about 40 small or 20 big mint leaves. Place in a small bowl. Cover with 3 ounces bourbon. Soak for 15 minutes. Then gather the leaves in paper towels. Wring the mint over the bowl of bourbon. Repeat the process several times.

TO MAKE THE MINT JULEP

1. Pour 3½ cups of bourbon into a large glass bowl or glass pitcher. Add 1 cup of simple syrup to the bourbon. Now add the mint extract 1 tablespoon at a time to the mixture until it tastes as you'd like it to (3 tablespoons is usually about right). Pour the whole mixture back into a bottle or pitcher and refrigerate it for at least 24 hours.

2. To serve the julep, fill each glass (ideally a silver mint julep cup) half full with shaved ice. Insert a spring of mint and then more ice until the ices sits about 1 inch over the top of the cup. Then insert a straw (it's best if you cut the straw to 1 inch above the top of the cup). Pour the refrigerated julep mixture over the ice. Add a sprinkle of powdered sugar to the top of the ice.

Paprika-Dusted Deviled Eggs

From the kitchen of Annie Campbell

1 dozen large eggs

¼ cup good mayonnaise, such as Hellman's or Best Foods

2 teaspoons Dijon mustard

¼ teaspoon salt

¼ teaspoon hot sauce

Hot paprika

1. Fill a large mixing bowl with lots of ice and water and set aside.

2. Bring a large stockpot filled with about 4 inches of water to a rolling boil. Using a slotted spoon, carefully lower the eggs into the boiling water. After 14 minutes, transfer to the ice bath with the slotted spoon. When completely cool, drain and carefully peel off the shells, taking care not to tear the egg whites. Rinse off any bits of shell and pat dry.

3. Slice the eggs in half lengthwise and remove the yolks, placing them in a medium bowl with the mayonnaise, mustard, salt, and hot sauce. Mash with a fork until smooth. Spoon the yolk mixture back into the egg halves (or pipe the yolk mixture into the cavity of each white). Garnish each half with a dusting of paprika. Serve in a deviled egg dish.

Kentucky Hot Brown Bites

From the kitchen of Annie Campbell

Cooking spray

1½ (5 oz.) containers finely shredded Parmesan cheese

1⅔ cups milk

¼ cup butter

3 tablespoons all-purpose flour

2 ounces medium cheddar cheese, shredded (about ¼ cup)

¼ teaspoon kosher salt

¼ teaspoon freshly ground pepper

4 ounces thinly sliced deli turkey cut into 2-inch squares

4 cooked bacon slices, crumbled

½ cup diced fresh tomato

Fresh flat-leaf parsley leaves for garnish

1. Preheat the oven to 350°F.

2. Line 2 baking sheets with aluminum foil and lightly coat with cooking spray. Spoon the Parmesan cheese by tablespoons ½ inch apart onto prepared baking sheets, forming 12 (2½-inch) rounds on each sheet.

3. Bake 1 sheet at 350°F for 7 to 9 minutes or until the edges of the mounds are lightly browned and beginning to set. Working quickly, transfer the cheese rounds to a lightly greased (with cooking spray) 24-cup miniature muffin pan, pressing gently into each cup to form shells. Repeat the procedure with the second baking sheet.

4. Microwave the milk in a microwave-safe measuring cup for 30 seconds on high or until warm. Melt the butter in a small saucepan over medium-high heat. Whisk in the flour; cook, whisking constantly, for 1 minute. Gradually whisk in the warm milk. Bring to a boil, whisking constantly, for 1 to 2 minutes, or until thickened. Whisk in the cheddar cheese, kosher salt, and black pepper.

5. Increase the oven temperature to 425°F. Line each Parmesan shell with 2 turkey pieces and fill each with 1 teaspoon cheese sauce. Bake for 5 minutes. Remove from the pan to a wire rack and top with crumbled bacon and diced tomato. Garnish with flat-leaf parsley leaves.

Chocolate Derby Pecan Pie

From the kitchen of Annie Campbell

3 large eggs, slightly beaten

¼ pound (1 stick) unsalted butter, melted

⅔ cup all-purpose flour

¾ cup sugar

¼ cup brown sugar

1 teaspoon cinnamon

2 teaspoons pure vanilla extract

1 cup semisweet chocolate chips

½ cup chopped pecans

½ cup chopped walnuts

One 9-inch prebaked Annie's Pie Crust (recipe follows) or prebaked store-bought pie crust

Whipped cream or ice cream for topping (optional)

This pie may be made a day or two in advance, covered, and refrigerated. Double the filling to make two pies. You'll be happy you did!

1. Preheat the oven to 350°F.

2. Whisk together the eggs, melted butter, flour, sugar, brown sugar, cinnamon, and vanilla extract until smooth. Stir in the chocolate chips, pecans, and walnuts. Spread the mixture into the prepared pie crust.

3. Bake for 35 minutes, or until the filling is set and the top and crust are golden brown. Serve with whipped cream or ice cream, if desired.

Annie's Pie Crust

2½ cups all-purpose flour

2 tablespoons sugar

1 teaspoon kosher salt

2½ sticks very cold unsalted butter, cut into ¼-inch pats

6 tablespoons to ½ cup cold water

1. Combine two-thirds (about 1⅔ cups) of the flour with the sugar and salt in the bowl of a food processor. Pulse to incorporate. Spread the butter chunks evenly over the surface. Pulse until no dry flour remains and the dough just begins to form clumps, or about 25 short pulses. Use a rubber spatula to spread the dough evenly around the bowl of the food processor. Sprinkle with the remaining flour and pulse until the dough is just barely broken up, about 5 short pulses.

2. Transfer the dough to a large bowl. Sprinkle the dough with water; then, using a rubber spatula, fold and press it until it comes together into a ball. Divide the ball in half. Form each half into a 4-inch disk. Wrap tightly in plastic and refrigerate for at least 2 hours or freeze for up to 3 months.

3. On a well-floured work surface, using a rolling pin dusted with flour, roll out the chilled dough into a 12-inch round. Transfer the dough to a pie pan. Press the dough evenly into the pan and use your preferred crimping technique to decorate the edge of the crust. Place the pan in the freezer for 2 hours before baking.

4. Preheat the oven to 375°F.

5. Remove the pie crust from the freezer and line the inside with parchment paper. Place pie weights (or dried beans) on top of the parchment paper to weigh down the crust. Bake for 15 minutes. Remove from the oven and remove the parchment paper and weights. Return the pan to the oven to bake for 10 minutes more, or until the crust starts to turn golden brown. Remove from the oven and let cool until ready to use.

Cheekwood

A very fancy, old-time fund-raising ball is held every year at Cheekwood, a historic estate in Nashville set on fifty-five acres that includes a vast botanical garden. I've always loved Cheekwood, which was donated to the city by the Cheek family. They amassed a fortune from their grocery empire, including Maxwell House coffee (remember "Good to the last drop"?). My grandmother and I often met for lunch or teatime in Cheekwood's Pineapple Room, which has long been the place in town for the ladies-who-lunch set. Every time we went, we were guaranteed to see half a dozen ladies Dorothea knew.

On holiday breaks as a teenager, I served as a docent at Cheekwood. From Thanksgiving to New Year's Day, the "Trees of Christmas" exhibit featured fir trees decked out by local businesses in different themes, such as Visions of Sugar Plums or Christmas Around the World. It was my job to guide people through the exhibit and explain why a decoration had been chosen by a tree's designer. I loved it because I got to pretend I was an art historian in a fancy museum . . . did I mention I was a huge nerd?

Equestrian Transferware

Growing up, I found that nearly every Nashville dining room I walked into had steeplechase-themed wallpaper. My grand-mother took the trend to heart. She had the wallpaper— and the dishes. She loved a horse theme, particularly when it came to her antique English transferware.

Transferware is a kind of ceramics made using transfer printing that dates to eighteenth-century England and usually has a country scene in white and blue or white and red. Once you get into a pattern, you can get addicted to collecting it. Dorothea eventually owned every piece in her pattern's set, from dinner plates and teacups to platters and bowls, plus a big soup tureen and ladle that my dad and I stumbled upon while rummaging around the flea market at the Fairgrounds Nashville early one Saturday morning. That piece became the focal point of her dining room— often spilling over with fresh peonies from her backyard garden.

To this day, transferware is my favorite item to hunt for at a flea market. I always feel as though I've hit the lottery when I find a piece of cranberry-colored transferware that Dorothea would have loved—with a horse on it, of course!

Steeplechase

The Iroquois Steeplechase horse race has been a Nashville tradition for more than seventy-five years. It's a great excuse to put on a pretty dress and have some fun. Seersucker, linen, bow ties, pocket squares, embellished hats, and wacky fascinators—it's all fair game at Steeplechase.

Every year, my parents and their friends would get together at someone's home for cocktails before taking a picnic of pulled pork sliders to the track.

MENU

steeplechase picnic menu

Pulled Pork Sliders with Bourbon
BBQ Sauce and Pickled Red Onions

The Mockingbird:
Sorghum Old-Fashioned Cocktail

Pulled Pork Sliders with Bourbon BBQ Sauce and Pickled Red Onions

From the kitchen of Annie Campbell

⅓ cup salt

⅓ cup brown sugar

1 tablespoon smoked paprika

2 teaspoons ground cumin seeds

2 teaspoons espresso powder

3 cloves garlic, minced

5 pounds boneless pork shoulder

1 to 1½ cups Bourbon BBQ Sauce (recipe follows)

24 mini brioche buns, halved

Butter for toasting brioche buns

2 cups Pickled Red Onions (recipe follows)

Make the barbecue sauce and pickled onions the week before to get a jump start on this classic Derby recipe. The pork shoulder can be cooked and shredded up to 2 days in advance, then stored in an airtight container in the refrigerator.

1. Combine the salt, brown sugar, paprika, cumin, espresso powder, and garlic. Rub the mixture all over the pork. Wrap the pork tightly with plastic wrap and refrigerate overnight or up to 24 hours.

2. Preheat the oven to 250°F. Unwrap the pork and place it in a roasting pan. Cook in the preheated oven for 4 hours, basting with the rendered fat and juices every hour. After 4 hours, or when an instant-read thermometer registers an internal temperature of 150°F, remove the pork from the oven and wrap tightly in aluminum foil. Return the wrapped shoulder to the oven and cook for 4 hours more.

3. Remove the pork shoulder from the oven and let it rest. When cool enough to handle, shred the meat into thin strands with your hands. Pour ½ cup of the pan juices over the pork and stir in ¾ to 1 cup of Bourbon BBQ Sauce. Taste for seasoning and add more sauce or pan juices, as desired.

TO MAKE THE SLIDERS

Preheat the broiler. Butter the cut sides of the brioche buns and toast under the broiler. Pile hot pulled pork onto the bottom half of the slider bun and top with a few slices of Pickled Red Onions. Secure the top half of the bun using a knotted bamboo skewer or a toothpick, and serve immediately!

Bourbon BBQ Sauce

From the kitchen of Annie Campbell

1½ cups chicken stock

2 tablespoons Kentucky bourbon or Tennessee whiskey, depending on your team

1 cup ketchup

½ cup dark molasses

1 tablespoon plus 1 teaspoon onion powder

2 teaspoons garlic powder

½ teaspoon ground cumin

½ teaspoon freshly ground black pepper

½ teaspoon kosher salt

¼ cup Worcestershire sauce

2 tablespoons Dijon mustard

¼ cup red wine vinegar

1 tablespoon plus 1 teaspoon hot sauce, plus more to taste

1 tablespoon liquid smoke

1. Whisk together all the sauce ingredients in a small saucepan over medium-low heat.

2. Simmer until reduced to a glaze consistency, about 15 minutes (the sauce should reduce by about one-third).

3. Adjust the flavor with more molasses, vinegar, or hot sauce to taste. Cooled barbecue sauce can be stored in a sealed container in the refrigerator for several months.

Pickled Red Onions

From the kitchen of Annie Campbell

3 cups water

2 tablespoons kosher salt

3 tablespoons sugar

½ cup red wine vinegar

1 red onion, sliced paper thin

Use a mandoline to slice the onions superthin in a flash. These onions get tastier the longer they pickle, so it is best to make them well in advance and store them in the refrigerator.

1. Combine the water, salt, and sugar in a medium saucepan.

2. Heat over medium heat until the salt and sugar are fully dissolved.

3. Remove from heat and let cool. Stir in the vinegar.

4. Pour the vinegar mixture over the onions, transfer to a clean quart-sized jar, and store in the refrigerator until ready to use.

The Mockingbird
Sorghum Old-Fashioned Cocktail

2 ounces sorghum whiskey or your favorite whiskey

¼ to ½ ounce simple sorghum syrup (recipe follows)

2 to 3 dashes Angostura bitters

1½-inch-long orange peel (orange part only)

The last time I was in Nashville, I went to a restaurant called the Mockingbird. (It serves these amazing things called "tatchos"—tater tots, lamb chili, beer cheddar, and scallions.) While there, I had one of the best old-fashioned cocktails of my life, which inspired me to do this southern riff on a classic cocktail when I came across some sorghum whiskey.

Sorghum is a type of grass that grows tall into canes with beautiful tassels on top. It grows well in the Tennessee plateau, and the canes can be pressed to extract juice, which is then boiled down to create sorghum syrup. It is a very old-fashioned technique, and although the texture and color of the syrup are similar to those of molasses, it has a very different taste. Muddy Pond sorghum syrup is grown and made in central Tennessee and is available online. That brand is also used in a wonderful sorghum whiskey made by High Wire Distilling Company.

In a mixing glass or small pitcher, combine the whiskey, simple sorghum syrup, and bitters and stir together. If you like to drink an old-fashioned "neat," add some ice to the pitcher and strain into a rocks glass. If you like to drink it with ice, pour into a rocks glass over ice. Hold the orange peel over the drink and twist it to express some of the flavorful oil into the glass, then drop the peel into the drink.

Simple Sorghum Syrup

½ cup sorghum syrup

½ cup water

In a small saucepot, heat the sorghum syrup and water together to a simmer—do not let it boil. Remove from the heat and allow to cool. Keep covered in the refrigerator for up to 1 month.

CHAPTER 11

Catching Frogs & Selling Lemonade

What I loved about being a child in the South was that we played outdoors all the time. Playing Atari games was a real treat, but most of our days were spent running around the neighborhood, riding our bikes, climbing trees, and getting covered in mud. I had one of those idyllic childhoods where I would get home at three o'clock, throw down my backpack, and run outside with my brother to join the neighborhood kids for kickball or tag until it got dark. Kids ran to one another's houses, shared one another's homes. There weren't a lot of rules, boundaries, or playdates. No one scheduled us. I learned about social dynamics by having to get along with whatever bunch of random kids happened to be outside on any given day. There was a creek that ran through our neighborhood. We would all walk down to the creek and catch crawdads or frogs. (To this day, if I see a frog I will chase it, to my husband's horror!)

In the evening, whenever our folks left the house, my brother and I would go on a mission to eat all the sweets we could find. John was the family spy. He always managed to see where my mom hid the best treats, and the minute the adults departed, we would find the stash. He would drag the big kitchen stool next to the fridge and climb up to get to Mom's "hidden" stash of M&M's or MoonPies. Joy was staying up past our bedtime, watching cartoons, hiding the empty candy bags behind the sofa cushions.

At the same time, we were expected to clean up nicely and to have impeccable manners in polite society.

We were taught to look people in the eye and to say hello and smile. Smiling at people is a big part of life in the South. If a child does not wave back at someone walking down the street, don't be surprised if the adult says, "Excuse me, little one. Where are your manners?"

Good manners take very little effort. It's not that hard to smile. My mother likes to say, "Smiles are contagious." Try smiling at people you don't even know for a day. Even if you're not in Nashville, most of them will smile back at you. It really does make a difference. Those little daily kindnesses, they can really change the mood of a block, a neighborhood, a city. My mother made sure we knew it was a necessity to be extra-nice to people doing the hard jobs that make other people more comfortable, like waiters, salespeople, and hotel workers. I love the way my husband is with people at a restaurant—in fact, I always observe how people act with waiters. It says a lot.

My kids sometimes meet hundreds of new people a week, because we have to travel so much for my work. I think there's something really great about their learning to look people in the eye, to introduce themselves, to be respectful, to take care of other people's property. We always say in the South that good manners are a kind of passport. If you have good manners, you can go everywhere and people are glad to have you around.

In this spirit, I grew up saying "Please" and "Thank you" and "Yes, ma'am" and "No, sir." It actually took a long time to drum that "ma'am" habit out of me. I had to live in California for at least fifteen years before I stopped calling women even five years older than me "ma'am." What can I say . . . it was a huge part of my upbringing!

We were taught manners by example. The older women in our families were unflappably polite. Southern women are strong and outspoken but also beautifully composed and always present their best selves to the world. They believe in character and the presentation of that character. They aren't afraid to tell you how they really feel.

Someone once told me they thought people in the South were passive-aggressive in their politeness. Certainly not! In my experience, a southern woman will tell you right to your face if she doesn't like something. If my mother or grandmother wasn't pleased with my behavior, she'd say, "I don't like that. The way you're behaving is ugly. I don't like when children behave ugly." I feared their disapproval, and one pointed look from either

How to Catch a Frog with Your Bare Hands

Step 1: Be quiet. You have to sneak up on a frog.

Step 2: Cheaters use nets. You want to use your hands. Grab the frog—fast!—by the legs with one hand. Support the rest of the frog with your other hand.

Step 3: Carry it around for a minute or two and show it off. Startle your parents—or, if you are me, your husband.

Step 4: Release back into the pond.

of them could terrify me. Getting a "Stop acting ugly" was just the worst! I hated disappointing my grandma or my mother.

But they also taught me to strive for behavior that was beautiful. And in my mother's and grandmother's eyes, what was beautiful was treating others with respect and putting your best foot forward. Taking care of your community was beautiful, as was doing nice things for others. My grandma always said, "Pretty is as pretty does." People aren't pretty if they act ugly.

One time my grandma caught me chewing gum. She said, "The only appropriate place to chew gum is behind a door." One time I really wanted to chew gum, so I went behind the door to do it, just to prove a point. But it made me realize that some people think it's rude to chew gum around them. I like gum. But I was able to see my grandmother's perspective: there is a time and a place for chewing gum, because, let's just face it, it can be a little gross watching other people chew.

Business Lessons

One other thing the South gave me as a child was a good work ethic. I had two business ventures as a young person, and both taught me lessons that I still put into practice today.

The first was a lemonade stand. I think a lemonade stand is a really good way for kids to learn about business. My brother and I took it very seriously. We would fill one of my mom's huge tea pitchers with ice-cold lemonade and set up our table with paper cups, napkins, and a Mason jar to hold our money.

John and I always fought about pricing. He is four years older and thought we should be charging more than I thought we should. We

would compromise on a quarter a cup, because we could take those quarters straight to the arcade afterward.

Creating the sign for the lemonade stand was my favorite part. Give me markers and some poster board, and I'm in my element. I also liked innovating: I'd find ways for our stand to be special, such as putting mint leaves in each cup, or having both iced tea and lemonade so people could create their own Arnold Palmer.

Being the loudmouth of the family, I was also the designated barker. I would flag down cars and harangue people into extra cups ("Doesn't your husband want a cup, too?"). My brother and I developed quite a reputation on our block for running a tidy business.

Our second venture was our more innovative by far. It all began in third grade with some hair clips. I spotted them at the mall. They were very cool and just fifty cents apiece, and they were glimmering with potential. I had my brother front me some money as an invest-

ment, so I could get a lot of them and some paint pens.

I wrote my name with paint pen on the barrettes, wore them to school, and waited for other girls to notice. It didn't take long. Soon they started asking me if I'd make them barrettes. Sure, I would: for $2. They would meet me at my desk before or after school, and in bubble letters I'd write their name or a chosen slogan in paint pen for a markup of $1.50. The orders poured in. It became like a status symbol: everybody had to have a hair clip. And so began my first real triumph in the entrepreneurial space.

I learned a lot of principles of business that way. I learned about pricing, and that margins are important. I learned that the customer is always right. If she didn't like the writing, I had to redo it and absorb the cost of the one that she didn't like. I learned that marketing is everything.

But I flew too close to the sun. I spent more time on my barrette business than on schoolwork, became a distraction to the girls around me, and got paint pen all over my desk. As a result, I got into a lot of trouble and my business was shut down by my third-grade teacher. Ah, the hazards of an elementary school start-up . . .

In both the lemonade-stand and barrette businesses, I loved learning about how business works. I was fascinated with the idea of turning a profit. I wasn't afraid of hard work, and I liked engaging the market. It made me understand supply and demand. Also, I did like making enough cash to maintain my very expensive sticker collection.

People of my generation might remember this phenomenon: We had books with all kinds of stickers, from scratch-and-sniff ones to shiny backs to puffy ones. Garfield. Peanuts. All of it. But the hardest to get, most desirable ones by far were Mystiks. They had a sort of plasma inside (some people called them "oilies") and usually had cosmic, dreamy themes, such as unicorns or wizards. A penguin with a bow tie. Butterflies! Sharks! Poodles! Hot-air balloons! They were a dollar each. A dollar!

All I can say is, it's good I was doing so well with my businesses, because I needed those stickers—bad. How 1980s businesspeople got kids addicted to stickers, I will never understand, but it was pretty pervasive.

The main thing I learned from all my entrepreneurial success was that working with my brother on the funding for the hair clip venture or on selling lemonade made those things more fun. To this day, it's important to me to really enjoy the people I work with. That's another thing that I learned way back in elementary school: Don't go into business with people you don't like, because you never know whether or not you'll be successful in the end, so it's important to enjoy the journey.

These days, I don't start a movie, a television show, or a business with people I'm not ready to spend a lot of time with, because, let's face it, if work is fun, it doesn't feel like work. For example, I always have the best time working on movies shot in the South that are about southern people. (I have been lucky enough to work in Tennessee, North Carolina, Arkansas, Texas, Georgia, South Carolina, and West Virginia.) Plus, it's nice when I get to be on a movie set and talk in my native accent. I feel like I'm putting on an old pair of slippers that fit just right.

Lemonade-Stand Lemonade

12 lemons

1 cup sugar

6 cups cold water

Note: Heating lemon zest with the sugar and water boosts the lemony flavor.

1. Finely grate the zest of two of the lemons. Place the zest and sugar into a small saucepan with one cup of the water. Bring to a boil over high heat and reduce to a simmer. Stir until the sugar dissolves. Remove from heat and let stand for 10 minutes.

2. While the sugar syrup cools, juice the lemons (you should have about 1 cup fresh lemon juice). Place the juice in a gallon-sized jar. Pour the cooled syrup into the jar through a mesh strainer. Discard the solids. Pour the cold water into the jar and top with a tight-fitting lid. Shake well to combine. Chill until ready to use. Serve over ice. Adjust the sugar to sweeten to your liking.

The Dog House

While we're on the subject of children, I must say I'm very much in favor of children having pets. I myself am partial to dogs. Some of my favorite acquaintances are dogs! I have had many and often name them after famous figures, such as Coco Chanel. My mother started out with Yorkshire terriers named Cricket and Mr. Leo. The next dog was Sarah, my tiny black teacup poodle. For Christmas when I was five, I chose her over a bike. Then we had a dachshund named Boo-Boo. Then another Yorkie named Dixie, who ended up being toothless and bald, which was a real tragedy, though she took it in stride. My mother loved her dearly. I wasn't as big a fan. Then I had a Chihuahua named Chi-Chi. (That was even before I was in the movie *Legally Blonde*. Bizarre coincidence, right?) Then I had an English Bulldog named Frank Sinatra. (I am personally obsessed with bulldogs, and the University of Georgia Bulldogs mascot, Uga, happens to be the most adorable English bulldog you've ever seen. Of all the mascots of all the SEC teams, he's my favorite. You can't be sad watching Uga drool on his little red sweater.)

These days, we have a French bulldog named Pepper; Hank Williams, a chocolate Lab; and a German shepherd named Nashville, whom I call "The Sheriff." That's because he's the law around these parts. Growing up, I always dreamed of having a bunch of dogs around, and now I do. I don't even mind that my house smells like a kennel . . . Well, maybe I mind a little. I consider myself lucky that my husband loves dogs, too!

Honestly, everybody in the South talks about their dogs as if they were members of the family, and the dogs run wild there. Dogs have

OPPOSITE Doesn't a house feel more like a home with a dog waiting on the doorstep for you?

the best life in the South, because you just don't ever put a dog behind a fence. You wouldn't do that to someone in your family, and you certainly wouldn't do that to the family pet. Dogs wandered free around my neighborhood, no leashes or enclosures. Jubilee, our neighbors' dog, would come over and hang out at our house all the time, and no one thought it was strange. We played with the dogs as much as we played with other kids. They were part of our community.

Dogs were always just *around*. On mornings my parents drove car pool, every one of my friends would run out to the car with some sort of hunting dog as their escort. There were always dogs chasing the car back down the drive and running around the neighborhood as though they owned it.

My mother always said you need a dog to teach you responsibility, but I don't think that's the main lesson dogs have for us. I think they help us understand unconditional love and that humans aren't the only beings in the universe. Dogs bring out our compassion—something that's much needed in the world right now. They provide us with companionship and acceptance. I mean, what's better than chasing a dog? Or a dog chasing you? Or making another little creature happy? We get so much love and joy from spending time with our dogs.

Truthfully, we spoil our dogs to no end. They watch TV with us. My dogs hit the dog lottery. For example, I would never stop our chocolate Lab from rolling in the mud and then getting into the pool and then rolling in mud again and then coming inside. Because he's our *dog*. It's my philosophy that a dog can't be made to not get up on the furniture, and so the furniture must be dog-proof. We adapt to dogs rather than expecting them to behave like something other than what they are.

I've been blessed with so many really special animals in my life. Don't even get me started about horses. When I was a girl, I rode horses one summer at camp and learned how to take care of them. It was a lot of work, but my mom thought it was important for children to learn some manual labor. Even if I did get stomped on and bucked off too many times, I always got right back on the next day. And there has been a payoff: as it turns out, I'm always riding in movies and in photo shoots, and it's fun for me rather than scary. I must project an air of confidence on the sets, because no one ever hesitates to stick me on a horse or hand me a baby. I can't complain. I like horses, and I like babies.

Once I even got to work with an elephant. It was a magical experience. She communicated like a human being, I swear. It's such a privilege for me to be close to animals and get to work with them, because my grandma always used to say—and I say this to my kids all the time—you have to treat God's innocent creatures with kindness. Just because they can't speak, it doesn't mean they don't have feelings. A big part of growing up with respect for animals is letting the joy of having an animal into your life. It's a really beautiful thing for kids. It gives you deep compassion.

To this day, one question I find myself asking people is whether or not they've had that experience of bonding with an animal and feeling as though it had a human soul. The stories you hear! Almost all those I ask say there is or was a truly special animal in their life, usually a dog or a cat that they felt close to. I usually like those people best.

MENU

summer
porch picnic

When it comes to lazy summer days with kids and dogs running around, the best way to eat dinner is outside under tree cover or on the porch. In such weather, no one says no to a picnic, especially if we're talking about my grandmother's fried chicken (just as good cold as hot!), okra, and squash.

Dorothea's Corn Salad

Dorothea's Brined-and-Battered
Fried Chicken

Summer Squash Casserole

Fried Okra

Tutti-Frutti Ice Cream

Dorothea's Corn Salad

¼ cup white wine vinegar

2 tablespoons fresh lime juice (from 1 lime)

2 teaspoons Dijon mustard

1 teaspoon kosher salt

¼ teaspoon freshly ground black pepper

½ teaspoon honey

1 shallot, finely chopped

½ cup extra-virgin olive oil

8 ears corn, shucked, kernels removed (about 6 cups)

2 pints cherry tomatoes, halved

1 bunch green onions, white and light green parts only, thinly sliced

1 cup lightly packed fresh herb leaves, finely chopped; use a mix of whatever summer herbs you like best, such as basil, cilantro, chives, tarragon, and flat-leaf parsley

Dorothea was against two things: picking corn more than a day before you ate it and refrigerating a tomato. The natural sugars in sweet corn turn to starch soon after picking, so pick it or buy it from a farm stand the day you plan to cook it. Tomatoes get mealy and mushy when refrigerated, so keep them on a counter or windowsill until ready to use.

1. Combine the vinegar, lime juice, Dijon mustard, salt, pepper, honey, and shallot in a small jar and set aside for 10 minutes to allow the shallots to soften and flavor the vinegar. Add the oil, secure the lid on the jar, and shake vigorously for 30 seconds to emulsify the dressing.

2. Combine the corn, tomatoes, green onions, and herbs in a large bowl. Add the dressing and toss well to combine. Season the salad with more salt and pepper to taste. Serve at room temperature, or cover and chill until ready to serve.

Dorothea's Brined-and-Battered Fried Chicken

1 pint buttermilk mixed with ¼ cup hot sauce (optional)

One 1½- to 2-pound chicken, cut into 8 pieces

2 cups all-purpose flour

1 tablespoon kosher salt

1 tablespoon onion powder

1 tablespoon garlic powder

1 tablespoon hot paprika

1 tablespoon freshly ground black pepper

2 cups whole milk

2 large eggs, beaten

Peanut or vegetable oil for frying

Creamy Gravy (optional; recipe follows)

My grandmother made the best fried chicken. Going through family recipes, I found a tattered and splattered cookbook by Mrs. S. R. Dull called *Southern Cooking* and inscribed "Dorothea Witherspoon, May 14, 1942, Decatur, Georgia." Inside was a recipe for fried chicken with cream gravy, along with several index cards in my grandmother's handwriting for other versions of fried chicken. This recipe blends them all and is a great match for the fried chicken she made. Soaking the chicken pieces overnight in low-fat buttermilk mixed with your favorite hot sauce boosts flavor and tenderness. (Hot sauce has quite a bit of sodium in it, so it acts as a brine.) Double this recipe for hearty eaters.

1. Pour the buttermilk–hot sauce mixture into a large zip-lock bag, add the chicken pieces, seal, and place the bag in the refrigerator to let the chicken soak for at least 8 hours or up to 24 hours before frying. Set the bag aside to come to room temperature at least 30 minutes before frying. Drain in a colander, discarding the brine.

2. Combine the flour, salt, onion and garlic powders, paprika, and pepper in a heavy-duty paper bag. Whisk the milk and eggs together in a shallow dish. Drop several of the chicken pieces into the bag of seasoned flour, seal, and shake to coat the pieces thoroughly. Open the

Continued...

bag and dip the floured pieces in the egg wash. Return them to the bag of flour and shake to coat again. Set them aside on a wire rack while you repeat the process with the remaining pieces—flour, egg wash, flour.

3. Heat at least 3 inches of oil in a Dutch oven over medium-high heat until it reaches 325°F on a frying or candy thermometer. Carefully slip the chicken breast pieces, skin side down, into the hot oil. The oil temperature will drop. Regulate the heat to maintain a temperature of 325°F. Cook the breasts for about 7 minutes without moving them. Turn and cook for 7 to 8 minutes more without disturbing them.

The chicken is cooked when it reaches 160°F on an instant-read thermometer. Add the legs and thighs and fry, undisturbed, for about 8 to 10 minutes, turning once halfway through cooking. Maintain the temperature of the oil and fry the chicken until the meat is cooked through and reaches an internal temperature of 160°F.

4. Remove the fried chicken to a clean rack set over a paper towel–lined sheet pan to soak up excess grease. Season with salt and pepper while hot, if desired. If making the gravy, reserve 2 tablespoons of the grease from the frying pan. Serve the chicken warm or at room temperature.

Creamy Gravy

2 tablespoons grease from frying the chicken

2 tablespoons butter

¼ cup all-purpose flour

1 cup chicken stock

1 cup heavy cream

Kosher salt

Freshly ground black pepper

Place 2 tablespoons hot grease from frying the chicken in a small skillet over medium-high heat. Add the butter and, when the foam subsides, sprinkle the flour over the hot fat, whisking constantly, to make a roux. Cook until the roux is golden brown, about 1 minute. Whisk in the chicken stock and cream. Stir until smooth and thickened, 5 minutes more. Add salt and pepper to taste. Transfer to a warm gravy boat for serving.

Summer Squash Casserole

3 tablespoons olive oil

1 white onion, chopped

2 garlic cloves, minced

1½ pounds yellow squash, sliced

1½ pounds zucchini, sliced

2 teaspoons salt

3 tablespoons butter

24 Ritz crackers

1 cup shredded sharp cheddar cheese

2 large eggs beaten with ½ cup heavy cream

1 teaspoon sugar

1 teaspoon salt

½ teaspoon freshly ground black pepper

3 tablespoons finely grated Parmesan cheese

2 tablespoons chopped fresh parsley

My granddad always grew squash in his summer garden, so my grandma would whip up some type of squash dish every night for months. This was one of our favorites.

1. Preheat the oven to 375°F. Lightly grease a 2-quart baking dish.

2. Heat the olive oil in a large skillet over medium-high heat. Add the onion and sauté 3 minutes. Add the garlic to the onions and sauté 1 minute more. Add the yellow squash and zucchini to the pan with the salt; sauté for 8 to 10 minutes, or until just tender. Transfer the squash to a colander to drain away excess moisture. Add the butter to the hot pan to melt and remove the pan from the heat.

3. Place the crackers in a large zippered bag, seal, and roll over them with a rolling pin, or a juice glass on its side, to create coarse crumbs. Transfer half of the crumbs, along with the drained squash, to a large mixing bowl. Combine ¾ cup of the cheddar cheese, the egg-cream mixture, and the sugar, salt, and pepper and gently fold the mixture into the squash and crumbs. Transfer the squash mixture to the prepared baking dish.

4. Combine the remaining cracker crumbs with the melted butter, the remaining ¼ cup cheddar, and the Parmesan. Sprinkle the mixture over the top of the casserole. Bake for 20 to 25 minutes. Remove from the oven and sprinkle with parsley.

Fried Okra

2 pounds fresh okra pods

Vegetable oil

½ cup yellow cornmeal

¼ cup all-purpose flour

½ cup kosher salt

½ teaspoon freshly ground black pepper

½ teaspoon garlic powder

Pinch of cayenne pepper

Kosher salt to taste

At my grandparents' house, we had to work for our dinner. My grandmother would take the okra we'd just picked, slice it into thin coins, and fry them up in her little deep fryer in the kitchen. Yes, she had her own mini deep fryer! Odd as it may sound, okra remains my favorite vegetable to this day.

1. Wash the okra well and drain. Cut off the tips and stem ends. Slice the okra crosswise into ½-inch slices.

2. In a Dutch oven, heat 2 inches of oil over medium-high heat to 350°F.

3. While the oil heats, combine the cornmeal, flour, salt, pepper, garlic powder, and cayenne pepper in a wide, shallow bowl. Roll the damp okra slices in the cornmeal mixture to coat. Carefully drop the okra into the hot oil and cook until golden brown, about 1½ to 2 minutes on each side. Remove with a slotted spoon to a paper towel–lined plate to drain. Season lightly with salt, if desired.

Tutti-Frutti Ice Cream

**FOR THE
ICE CREAM BASE**

1 quart (4 cups)
heavy cream

½ cup sugar

2 vanilla beans, split

Finely grated zest of
1 orange (about
2 tablespoons)

Pinch of salt

**FOR THE FRUIT
MIX-INS**

½ cup drained preserved
cherries, coarsely
chopped (to class it up,
try Luxardo gourmet
maraschino cherries in
place of the usual dyed
variety)

1 (8 oz.) can pineapple
tidbits, drained

5 apricot halves in syrup
(half of a 15.3-ounce
can), drained and
coarsely chopped

Most Sundays, my grandfather made tutti-frutti ice cream in a hand-cranked ice cream maker filled with ice and rock salt. He'd have us crank the machine on the porch. We'd fight over churning duty, eager to get the dessert done as soon as possible. The ice cream base does not use eggs, so it's a bit lighter. It also freezes harder than custard-based ice cream, so let it sit at room temperature for about 10 minutes for easier scooping. You can also soften your favorite vanilla ice cream and stir in the fruit to make quick tutti-frutti.

1. Combine 1 cup of the cream and the sugar in a saucepan over low heat. Scrape the seeds from the split vanilla beans and stir into the cream along with the scraped pods, orange zest, and salt. Stir until the sugar dissolves, then remove the pan from the heat. Let sit for 15 minutes. Discard the vanilla bean pods and stir in the remaining cream and refrigerate until thoroughly chilled.

2. Churn the chilled cream in a 2-quart ice cream maker for 5 minutes according to the manufacturer's instructions. Stop churning and add the chopped fruit. Continue churning until the ice cream is ready, about 10 to 12 minutes more. Serve straight from the machine, or transfer to a freezer container and freeze for up to 3 months.

CAFE

HOT BISCUITS COUNTRY HAM

Loveless

MOTEL

AIR CONDITIONED

NO VACANCY

CHAPTER 12

Road Trip!

One thing to remember about summer in the South: it's *hot*. Really, really hot. When I was a kid, I'd hope to get invited somewhere with a pool or I'd sit in a kiddie pool in the yard. Still, when even the ceiling fans and sweet tea weren't doing the trick, it was almost mandatory to take refuge. For my family, that almost always meant climbing into the car and driving some- where, preferably to a body of water or to an air-conditioned movie theater or out to eat somewhere in the country or to go explore our glorious national and state parks, such as Cummins Falls State Park in Tennessee. And all along the highways, you'd see signs for the famously well-advertised Lookout Mountain roadside attraction Rock City.

I'll never forget riding around in my dad's 1976 Cadillac El Dorado convertible. It was the smoothest ride, like cruising on the ocean in a boat. We used it for road trips and for Sunday drives out to this quaint diner attached to a country motel called

Hot Chicken

When I was growing up, I knew of only one place that served Nashville Hot Chicken: Prince's Hot Chicken Shack. Spicy-food junkies came for miles to eat there and to argue with one another about which was better: Prince's in Nashville or Gus's World Famous Fried Chicken in Memphis. I'm happy to say that both Prince's and Gus's seem to be going strong to this day. And they are both must-visits. Now, hot chicken is literally the most delicious thing you've ever had. And you can take my word for that because as a rule I don't even like spicy food. Nevertheless, hot chicken is impossible to turn down. And I'm happy to see that new hot chicken places are opening all the time these days. Not long ago I got to visit Hattie B's in Nashville, which serves chicken with just the perfect amount of spice and flavor to make your mouth feel like it's actually on fire. You need a glass of milk after every serving.

the Loveless Cafe. It's thirty minutes outside Nashville. They serve the best hot biscuits and world-class country ham, not to mention collard greens, macaroni, fresh-made jam, and country-fried cube steak with gravy. Not exactly diet food, but well worth every single calorie.

All over the South people stop for a meal at these sorts of restaurants. They're called meat-and-threes, because you pick three vegetables to go with your fried chicken, smothered pork chop, or meat loaf. The rare southern vegetarian will stick to a veggie plate alone. Speaking of which, northerners are sometimes surprised to see mac-'n'-cheese or corn bread on the list of "vegetable" sides. Accept it: carbs are a major food group in the South.

The Cadillac is the quintessential southern road trip car, and it's been that way for generations. I think that's because it's so comfortable, like sitting on a sofa. When my grandmother was a little girl, she and her parents drove in their Cadillac from Tennessee to Florida every summer. (I have a picture of my grandma young in her bathing costume looking beyond chic!) Then, when she became a mother with her own Cadillac, every March she would drive my dad and his brother down to Daytona Beach. And then my dad took me and my brother on road trips in *his* Cadillac. On those vacations, we would sometimes even forgo a hotel so we could sleep in the car. It was so big, we didn't mind.

Road Trip Playlist

"I GOT YOU (I FEEL GOOD)"

JAMES BROWN

"ON YOUR WAY"

ALABAMA SHAKES

"HAPPY TRAILS"

ROY ROGERS

"ON THE ROAD AGAIN"

WILLIE NELSON

"THIS LAND IS YOUR LAND"

WOODY GUTHRIE

"ANGEL FROM MONTGOMERY"

BONNIE RAITT

"I'VE BEEN EVERYWHERE"

JOHNNY CASH

"AFTER YOU'VE GONE"

BESSIE SMITH

"AMARILLO BY MORNING"

GEORGE STRAIT

"MY SILVER LINING"

FIRST AID KIT

"THE GAMBLER"

KENNY ROGERS

"PANCHO AND LEFTY"

MERLE HAGGARD & WILLIE NELSON

"EVERY DAY IS A WINDING ROAD"

SHERYL CROW

"COME TO MY WINDOW"

MELISSA ETHERIDGE

"THE WIND"

ZAC BROWN BAND

"ROUTE 66"

CHUCK BERRY

"VIVA LAS VEGAS"

ELVIS PRESLEY

"SOMEWHERE SOMEBODY"

AARON NEVILLE

"THE STORY"

BRANDI CARLILE

"PROUD MARY"

TINA TURNER

"A HORSE WITH NO NAME"

AMERICA

"GO YOUR OWN WAY"

FLEETWOOD MAC

"LOOKIN' OUT MY BACK DOOR"

CREEDENCE CLEARWATER REVIVAL

"BIG ROCK CANDY MOUNTAIN"

HARRY McCLINTOCK

Road Trip Games

I SPY: The person whose turn it is chooses an item within view and without signaling what it is says, "I spy something . . ." and then names the color, like "I spy something red!" The other people take turns guessing what it is. ("Dad's glasses case!" "My hair!" "That car's taillight!") Because it has to stay in view the whole time you're playing, this is ideal for pit stops, like when you're waiting for food to come at a restaurant, but on the road you can make rules about how, say, the item has to be inside of the car. Everyone takes a turn being the I-spy-er.

THE LICENSE PLATE GAME: Everyone seems to have a different version of this, but here's mine: You each get out a piece of paper and a pencil and write down all the states you see license plates from, keeping track of how many you see of each. When time's up (either when you stop for gas or when some time limit you've set runs out), you tally what you have, getting a point for every plate from the state you're in, two points for states that touch that state, and more (predetermined) points for states farther away. We ranked western states extrahigh, so if you could find one from California, you basically won.

THE ALPHABET GAME: This is a collaborative game. Looking out the window, you try to find (on street signs, license plates, billboards) all the letters in the alphabet, in order. So someone sees a sign for "Entering Alabama" and yells, "A-B!" Then someone sees a sign that says, "Car Parking" and says, "C!" And so on, until you get a hard letter, such as J or Z, and have a quiet few minutes searching.

Just to clarify: In the 1950s and '60s, Daytona wasn't a wild spring break destination. Back then, it was just the place everybody in Nashville wanted to take their kids for spring break or for a couple of weeks during the summer. And there was never a question about how you'd get there: of course you'd drive.

That's something very southern: people don't take airplanes if they can possibly help it. It doesn't matter if it's a three-hour drive or a fifteen-hour drive: they will get into the car. Still, to this day, my brother will pack his kids into the car with his wife and drive across several states to go on vacation. We don't do that in California. That's right, I've mostly succumbed: if I have to go to San Francisco, six hours away, I will get on a one-hour flight. And I do go in for more fuel-efficient vehicles now, though I still get awfully sentimental over those old Cadillacs.

I still love taking my kids for a road trip whenever possible. I think it's good for them. A road trip teaches you good, old-fashioned patience. The moral is: to get somewhere great, you have to put in the hours. The anticipation is exciting, and

you're so appreciative when you arrive. A road trip also lets you see just how vast and beautiful this country is and how many different ways people live.

What's more, a road trip is all about family togetherness, whether having long talks, playing car games, or listening to loud music. For my family, the music has always been a big part of that. My dad loved Guns N' Roses' *Appetite for Destruction*, the Steve Miller Band, Tom Petty, Creedence Clearwater Revival, Fleetwood Mac . . . those types of bands are the soundtrack of my childhood. My father also played a ton of James Brown on road trips. When I hear "I Feel Good," I can almost feel the wind in my hair.

Southern Cinema

Northerners might not associate movies with cars, but where I come from we got into the Cadillac to go see a movie—ideally at a drive-in (there are still a few of these left in Tennessee!).

And while we're talking film, how great is it that so many classic films have been made in or about the South over the years? Here are some of them. If you can't get to a drive-in movie theater, I highly recommend movie nights at home with friends or family and a big bowl of buttered stove-top popcorn, whatever the weather.

FORREST GUMP

GONE WITH THE WIND

TO KILL A MOCKINGBIRD

THE HELP

A TIME TO KILL

O BROTHER, WHERE ART THOU?
(Does it get any better than this soundtrack?)

DIVINE SECRETS OF THE YA-YA SISTERHOOD

STEEL MAGNOLIAS

THELMA AND LOUISE

TERMS OF ENDEARMENT

SWEET HOME ALABAMA (a shameless plug)

DRIVING MISS DAISY

THE SECRET LIFE OF BEES

WALK THE LINE (another shameless plug)

FRIED GREEN TOMATOES

SELMA

HUSTLE & FLOW

RAY

FRIDAY NIGHT LIGHTS

CAT ON A HOT TIN ROOF

THE BLIND SIDE

CHAPTER 13

The Perfect Book Club

From the minute I could read, I always had my nose in a book. Every year when we got out of school in May for the summer, we would receive a summer reading list, and there'd be two required-reading books and five optional books. I wanted them all, and my grandmother would buy them for me. I spent lazy summers lying on the back porch of her house reading books that filled my summers with imagination and creative learning.

I love a great story—tales of adventure, historical fiction, mysteries. Reading is a relaxing escape to another world. Early on, Dorothea was the one who fostered a love of reading in John and me. Just as she'd done with my dad and uncle when they were young, she took us on outings to Nashville bookstores such as Davis-Kidd to browse the shelves and pick out a book. When I was really young, my grandmother read stories out loud to me in a very theatrical way.

Must-Read Books by Southern Authors

TO KILL A MOCKINGBIRD
BY HARPER LEE

THE SECRET HISTORY
BY DONNA TARTT

THE COLLECTED STORIES OF EUDORA WELTY
BY EUDORA WELTY

SING, UNBURIED, SING
BY JESMYN WARD

THE MEMBER OF THE WEDDING
BY CARSON McCULLERS

THE COMPLETE STORIES
BY FLANNERY O'CONNOR

THE MOVIEGOER
BY WALKER PERCY

I KNOW WHY THE CAGED BIRD SINGS
BY MAYA ANGELOU

BLOOD MERIDIAN
BY CORMAC McCARTHY

AS I LAY DYING
BY WILLIAM FAULKNER

ALL OVER BUT THE SHOUTIN'
BY RICK BRAGG

*QUEEN OF THE TURTLE DERBY
AND OTHER SOUTHERN PHENOMENA*
BY JULIA REED

She started with picture books, but by the time we were about four years old, she graduated us into chapter books. I would sit on her lap, and she would read in all the different voices and accents. She did A. A. Milne's *Now We Are Six* and Margery Williams's *The Velveteen Rabbit* with particular verve. I think watching her perform a book probably inspired me to become an actor. It also made me love reading, and fiction in particular.

Dorothea adored her book collection, and I'm fortunate enough to have some of her old first editions, including *East of Eden*. She read us some Jane Austen novels and a lot of southern literature, plenty of stories about little kids and their grandmas. She was a first-grade teacher, so she had all kinds of books around that were appropriate for kindergartners, but I just remember that she read and read and read to us. She always played music on her record player for us to dance to. And she had a lot of stories on the record player, so I could listen to Disney stories and follow along in the books.

Today, I consider books my friends. I love having them around, because they remind me of the times in my life when I was

THE GARDEN PARTY
KATHERINE MANSFIELD

PEARLS AND MEN
LOUIS KORNITZER

THE ROMANTIC EXILES
E.H. CARR

BRIGHTON ROCK
GRAHAM GREENE

CHARLES LAMB
ON ELIA

BIG QUESTIONS FROM LITTLE PEOPLE

THE HISTORY AND GENEALOGY OF THE WITHERSPOON FAMILY (1400-1972)   WITHERSPOON

MILNE · SHEPARD   Now We Are Six   DUTTON

MILNE · SHEPARD   When We Were Very Young   DUTTON

Charlotte's Web   E. B. White

ISLA FISHER   Marge in Charge   Piccadilly

The Wizard of Oz

M.A. LARSON   Pennyroyal Academy   Putnam

The Little Prince

E.L. Konigsburg   From the Mixed-up Files of Mrs. Basil E. Frankweiler   ATHENEUM

Holy Bible   New International Version   Hodman

ROALD DAHL   James and the Giant Peach   KNOPF

W. SOMERSET MAUGHAM   D. H. LAWRENCE   VIRGINIA WOOLF   DOUGLAS   BELL

BELL

Treasure Island

The Story of King Arthur and His Knights

THE PHANTOM TOLLBOOTH   NORTON JUSTER

DANNY the Champion of the WORLD

Betty, Mrs. Piggle Wiggle

A Christmas Carol and Other Christmas Writings   Charles Dickens

EYEWITNESS BOOKS

D'AULAIRES' BOOK OF GREEK MYTHS

reading them. I organize my books by color. I take the dust jacket off, and then I know where it belongs. If it's a white book, it goes in the white section. If it's red, it goes in the red section. I find those rows of books so pretty to look at, and it's also great because you do it once and then you're done. No constant realphabetizing or anything like that.

My favorite book is Graham Greene's *The End of the Affair*. I just love that book. He's such a beautiful writer. He'll break your heart. I also love Lorrie Moore. *Birds of America* was a really important book for me in my early twenties, because it was so insightful about how women make decisions and how we all have different attitudes toward relationships. Similarly, I find Ann Patchett's *This Is*

the Story of a Happy Marriage endlessly inspiring. When I read it, I feel like she's my smart, brilliant friend, and we're just having a conversation about life, marriage, divorce—all the big topics.

And then of course there's Donna Tartt's *The Secret History*, *The Little Friend*, and *The Goldfinch*. Authors who take the time and care to write about the details of life are so incredible to me. I have a deep appreciation for writers who are that observant and poignant.

The South has contributed a great deal to literature. I love Julia Reed's books. They have hilarious titles, such as *But Mama Always Put Vodka in Her Sangria!* I've been lucky enough to meet her in person. She sure knows how to spin a yarn, both at dinner parties and in her books. She knows the exact right moment to whisper a secret or a dirty joke. Then she laughs this magnificent laugh.

I love small, independent bookstores, such as Ann Patchett's Parnassus Books in Nashville. They create real community togetherness. There are also fantastic book festivals all over the South, such as the Southern Festival of Books in downtown Nashville, right in front of the Capitol Building. Small presses are

My Favorite English Teacher

Her name was Margaret Renkl, and in my junior year of high school she made me love literature. We had to read a lot of Shakespeare and *To Kill a Mockingbird*. It was a really formative year for me. I learned about character analysis, conflicts between characters, narrative structure, the journey of a hero and an antihero, and how to compare characters to real people in history. I really credit her with my early understanding of how to create a character as an actor. In a way she was my greatest acting teacher, because not only did she encourage my love of stories and reading, but she helped me learn to figure out how characters worked. We reconnected about ten years after I graduated from high school, and to this day we're in touch. We have a great email relationship. And she's a very dear friend of Ann Patchett. She isn't a teacher anymore, but she still writes, including for the *New York Times*. What a blessing to have such an engaged, encouraging, enthusiastic teacher in my life!

represented there, as well as best-selling authors.

Books make the best gifts, too. For children and adults alike, I love the Penguin Classics books. I think they're so beautiful, and they're a nice keepsake.

Recently, I've taken my love of books online with an Instagram book club that lets me share some of my favorites. Here are a few of my selections:

The Alice Network by Kate Quinn

The Lying Game by Ruth Ware

Little Fires Everywhere by Celeste Ng

The Rules of Magic by Alice Hoffman

The Last Mrs. Parrish by Liv Constantine

Braving the Wilderness by Brené Brown

The Light We Lost by Jill Santopolo

Erotic Stories for Punjabi Widows by Balli Kaur Jaswal

Happiness: A Memoir: The Crooked Little Road to Semi-Ever After
    by Heather Harpham

Offline, I get together with a group of friends for a regular Girls' Book Club Night. I cherish these evenings. Not only do they give us an excuse to read the same book so we have something specific to discuss, but then when we (inevitably) digress to topics such as our families and work, it feels sort of like passing notes at school.

Here's what I like to serve, in addition to the usual cheese plate.

the perfect book club menu

Red and white wine

Baked Brie

Hot Spinach–Artichoke Dip

Olive medley

Crackers, cheese, and fruit

Baked Brie

1 whole Brie round

2 tablespoons peach preserves (really, any kind of fruit preserves will work; you can see what fruit and pepper jellies are made locally)

⅛ teaspoon red pepper flakes

1 tablespoon dried apricots, chopped

½ cup chopped pecans

1 teaspoon honey

2 teaspoons whiskey

1 teaspoon balsamic vinegar

Creamy cheese topped with fruit-and-nut chutney is a classic combination, but I make it southern style by using spiced-up peach preserves. The dried apricots and chopped pecans provide texture, and the Tennessee whiskey and vinegar give a great little kick of acidity to the rich cheese and sweet topping.

1. Preheat the oven to 350°F.

2. Line a baking sheet with parchment and place the round of Brie on the paper.

3. Stir together the preserves, pepper flakes, apricots, pecans, honey, whiskey, and vinegar and spoon over the top of the cheese round.

4. Bake for 5 to 10 minutes, keeping an eye on the cheese as it heats. The topping will begin to run down the sides and the cheese itself will begin to look misshapen. The warming time will vary depending on the brand of cheese and how cold it is to begin with. It's easy for the cheese to melt completely and the topping to burn if you don't watch it carefully. Serve with an assortment of crackers, apple slices, or bread.

Hot Spinach–Artichoke Dip

½ cup grated Parmesan cheese, divided

1 cup frozen spinach, thawed, drained, and coarsely chopped

1 (14 oz.) can artichoke hearts, drained and coarsely chopped

4 ounces (½ cup) cream cheese, room temperature

½ cup sour cream

¼ cup mayonnaise

1 clove garlic, grated

¼ cup shredded mozzarella cheese

4 to 5 dashes of hot sauce (optional)

This dip is a beloved cocktail party standard across the United States, but the South will lay ownership to anything containing cream cheese and mayonnaise. Perhaps one of the easiest party dishes to make, it goes equally great with cheap beer or fine wine.

1. Preheat the oven to 350°F.

2. Spray a small baking dish with baking spray or rub with soft butter.

3. Mix ¼ cup of the Parmesan cheese together with the rest of the ingredients and spoon into the baking dish.

4. Sprinkle the remaining ¼ cup of Parmesan cheese over the top of the mixture.

5. Bake until it begins to bubble and the cheese starts to brown, about 20 to 30 minutes. Serve warm with crackers or bread.

CHAPTER 14

My Did-Do Language

& NOTES ON SOUTHERN CONVERSATION

Conversation seems like a lost art sometimes. One pet peeve I have is poor introductions. I learned as a child to introduce myself with my first and last names. Nowadays, people just say, "Hi!"

I mean, c'mon, say your name! You're not wearing a name tag. I don't care if you've met somebody fifteen thousand times, say your name! I say my name to people all the time and they go, "Uh, I know who you are." But it's a habit, and it's part of how I was raised: to say my first and last name every single time I meet someone. People shouldn't have to guess.

As a little girl, I was taught to answer the phone by saying "Hello! Witherspoon residence. Reese speaking." Then the person who called had the obligation to say hello and introduce him- or herself. At my grade school, we learned to take a proper message and to make pleasant conversation with whomever was at the other end of the line.

We were also taught that the caller always had to hang up the phone first. That's right: you can't hang up until the other person does, which leads to *looooong* conversations sometimes.

These days, I've relaxed a little bit. Now I might say, "Hi, I'm Reese." But I think it's essential to assume that people don't know your name. People have got a lot going on. They might not remember that they met you three years ago at a school fund raiser.

The worst version of not saying your name is when people say, "Do you remember where you met me?" or "I bet you don't remember where we met!"

What is this, a quiz show? Testing people's memories in this way sends panic into people's hearts and their brain freezes up. I'm so worried I'm going to disappoint you or seem rude. It's a game that makes nobody happy. Isn't the whole point of socializing to make people feel good and comfortable, not on their heels and defensive?

Once you say you give up, they always say something ridiculous like "Summer camp! When we were thirteen!"

Oh, boy! Now, how am I expected, with the amount of information I have had to take in since I was thirteen years old, to remember my old bunkmate?

Of course, if you're the host of a party, it's incumbent upon you to introduce everybody to everyone else. You can do it any way that makes you feel comfortable, but everyone at the gathering needs to be introduced. I like to ask people what their first job was or ask something that is germane to the occasion. At a friend's birthday party, I went around and asked everyone to share his or her very first memory of our friend. It was pretty special to hear all our first impressions of the same person.

Another skill I was taught in sixth grade is the art of conversation. If you find yourself in any social situation, it's important to be ready to ask a few thoughtful questions. I like questions like "What's your dream job?" "What did you think you were going to be when you were in third grade?" "How different is your life than how you imagined it?" "Who is your favorite Spice Girl?" "If you could have anyone at your birthday party, who would it be?"

Whenever my girlfriend from Chattanooga, Tennessee, has a party, she always makes each guest say something nice about the guest seated to his or her left. At her parties, you will notice a lot of people trying very hard not to sit with certain people on their left! Sometimes it's tough to say something nice about somebody you just met, but it forces you to say that, for example, he or she has a nice smile or a beautiful shirt. It's a great icebreaker.

Betty-isms

My mother, Betty, is about as wise a guru as I've encountered in this life. She does not tolerate whining or sad-sacking, yet she is infinitely compassionate, always eager to try to share some of the lessons she's gleaned from living a full life. You'll be having a normal, everyday conversation, and then all of a sudden she'll casually say something so smart and so true that it could be on a greeting card or in a fortune cookie—or tattooed on your skin. I've stopped short of writing them on my body, but I do keep them at the back of my mind and call on them often, especially when I am—or someone I love is—struggling. I call them "Betty-isms." Here are some of my favorites:

1. Your job is your life insurance.
2. If you want something done, do it yourself—or ask another woman.
3. If you want love and companionship, buy a dog.
4. A bigger house won't make you happier, you'll just have more to clean.
5. If you want to meet a man, go to Home Depot (or a sports bar).
6. You won't meet any friends on your couch.
7. To have a good friend, be a good friend.
8. If it looks like a duck and walks like a duck, it's probably a duck.
9. Don't put a fox in charge of a henhouse.
10. The best things in life are not things.

Southern Expressions You Need to Know

"MAKE A SOW'S EAR INTO A SILK PURSE"
Make the best of any situation

"PITCHING A HISSY FIT"
Having a temper tantrum

"MADDER THAN A WET HEN"
(Pretty obvious)

"CATTYWAMPUS" OR "WHOPPERJAWED"
Crooked

"HAD A SIT-TO"
Talked to someone sternly

"GAVE HIM (OR HER) WHAT FOR"
Yelled at someone angrily

"THAT DOG CAN'T HUNT"
That person is useless

"PIDDLIN'"
Pathetic

"I'M FIT TO BE TIED"
You've had enough

"BLESS YOUR HEART!"
This expression is quintessentially southern. It can mean a lot of different things, from "You poor thing" to "You can't help messing up, can you?" to "You're the best." Don't worry, the tone of voice will tell you which version is meant!

Another good question is "What's your secret talent?"

I have a good one that you might not guess right away: I'm an excellent bowler. I mean, I don't want to brag, but it's an objective fact. I have a gift. We bowled every Friday night as kids. Our dad took me and my brother to the bowling alley while our mom worked the night shift, and I practiced and practiced until I got *great*. And to this day, every time I find myself in a bowling alley it all comes back to me. Seriously, I have to tone it down for kids' parties so I don't crush the children's dreams.

Once you get started, it's easy to have a good party conversation because most people love to talk about themselves. If you're curious at all, you can find something interesting or valuable in anyone. My mother taught me this. She could talk to a brick wall for three and a half hours. When I was a kid, it used to drive me crazy. We would go to the grocery store. While the cashier would be ringing up the groceries, my mom would start chatting with her. Fifteen minutes later, I'd be like, "Mom, she doesn't really care what you think about the new hospital administrator or the cold snap or the football game! Let's go home so she can get back to doing her job."

But these days, I find it charming. My mother is such a good conversationalist that she can find a common interest with literally anybody, from a gas station attendant to a movie star, just because she has a deep interest in people's lives.

Talkin' Southern

Now: a word on the way we talk in the South. You know, when I was growing up, I had no idea that I had an accent. It wasn't until I started traveling that I began getting teased about the way I talked— and not just the twang but also the phrases. We have expressions and euphemisms that you don't hear anywhere else. They sound so normal to me, but I'll say them outside the context of the South, and people will look at me like I'm insane.

"Oh my gosh," I say all the time. "He was like a long-tailed cat in a room full of rockers."

"People don't have the sense God gave them."

"Fixing to" when you're about to do something.

And more than anything else, I double up on the verb "to do," as in "Yeah, he did do" or "You done did it."

My husband, who is from Pittsburgh, is like, "What are you *talking* about?" My kids call it my did-do language. They can't understand a word of it, but it makes perfect sense to me. I mean, why would you did do what you already did done?

A Pronunciation Key

Pimento cheese is a southern delicacy, but northerners almost always pronounce it wrong, as "Pah-mento." The real way to say it is "Puh-minna." And, while we're at it: it's pe-CAHN, not PEE-can; HEW-ston, not HOW-ston. A pen is a "pi-un." Here are a few others. When in doubt, add an extra syllable.

WORD	SOUTHERN PRONUNCIATION	WORD	SOUTHERN PRONUNCIATION
all	*awl*	barbed wire	*bob-ware*
battery	*bat-tree*	before	*be-fow-ah*
boil	*bol*	business	*bid-ness*
can't	*cain't*	chicken	*chick-un*
eat	*ate*	egg muffin	*egg-a-muffin*
fellow	*fellah*	fire	*faar*
fork	*fok*	four, for	*fow-wah*
Georgia	*Jawjuh*	get	*git*
get you	*gitcha*	going to	*gonna*
government	*gubbamint*	hair	*her*
heater	*hater*	isn't it	*idnit*
lawyer	*law-yer* or *loy-er*	like	*lack*
marry	*murry* or *mare*	mayonnaise	*may-uh-naze*
month	*mont*	oil	*ol*
on	*own*	peas	*pays*
red	*ray-ed*	said	*say-ed*
school	*schule*	shrimp	*shramp*
situation	*sichy-ayshun*	sore	*so-war*
spoon	*spu-un*	sure do	*shore doo*
tire	*tarre*	tired	*tarred*

CHAPTER 15

Why Southern Ladies Love Holidays

It is a universally acknowledged truth that southern women love holidays. Most ladies I know decorate for every season of the year, and some even switch out their china. Pretty much every female friend I can think of has boxes of Halloween, Easter, and Christmas decorations somewhere in her house. We love to decorate. Heck, we even decorate our *mailboxes* in the South.

Why do we like holidays so much? I actually think it's pretty profound: we like having things to look forward to—times that we know will be entirely about family and togetherness and the kids and the things that really matter. When you put out your pumpkins or your garlands or your flags, you get a rush of excitement. You know you're creating an opportunity to make

memories and setting the stage for family time, which can be so elusive in the rush of the day to day.

Do southern women sometimes encounter resistance in our efforts to make holidays special? Yes, we do.

For example, I take a family photo every single year, in October, for our Christmas card. For five or six years, my kids complained. I would always say, "One day you'll thank me for making all these memories for you." Now they're used to it and give in to the photo ritual with hardly a complaint. They have learned to submit to wearing whatever holiday sweater I give them, and yes, that is one of my proudest achievements as a military commander . . . I mean, as a southern mother. As long as it doesn't have a reindeer or a snowman on it, my troop will comply.

I believe in the ritual of taking those photos, because it's important for my kids to feel like part of a family unit. And even if they grumble about having to sit still in a sweater on a hot day every fall, I do believe that one day they'll look at those photos and realize that someone cared enough to take a picture of them every year. Children need to understand that they are part of a family connected by traditions—even if it may take them a little while to realize what holidays are really about . . .

That's right: making your mother happy.

Kidding aside, here are my favorite things about each major holiday.

Christmas

Nashville rarely has a white Christmas. When it does snow, it doesn't usually stay long, but at least for the day or two until it melts, the countryside is breathtakingly beautiful. And whatever the weather, Advent calendars go up on December first. Then one day that month, ideally on some afternoon when it's too cold or rainy for the kids to play outside, we will put on some carols and make some hot chocolate and have a gingerbread-house day.

I gave up trying to make the gingerbread from scratch after one very messy year. Broken pieces . . . runny icing . . . it was a disaster. After that I was like, *Screw it, I'm just buying the pre-made one.* But let's get real . . . it doesn't matter. It doesn't matter if you make it from ginger you grew yourself or if you buy the blank ones and decorate them. It matters that kids remember the tradition and they get to eat candy and make something crafty. Plus you get to display their artwork up on the kitchen counter. My mother did it with me and my brother, and now I do it with my kids.

So on a table you have the kids' gingerbread houses and the Advent calendar, and you have the tree covered in lights. But I feel that staircases need a little greenery, too. I love to decorate the bannister

The Nashville Hot Chocolate

One tradition I feel other towns could benefit from is the Nashville "Hot Chocolate." Every Christmas at school, you'd have a kind of grandparents' day, but we called it a Hot Chocolate. And when stores had open houses for the holiday season and served snacks, that would be a Hot Chocolate. And when you were having a housewarming party, that would be a Hot Chocolate. Basically we used "Hot Chocolate" as another term for "get-together." So if you're having a casual daytime party, you're having a Hot Chocolate. And what do you serve there? Of course, hot chocolate. But you also have to serve hot apple cider, because sometimes you will get an oddball who doesn't like hot chocolate.

with a garland of magnolia and pine. And I clip Christmas cards onto the garland with clothespins. As you go up the stairway, you get to see all your friends' little children's faces on those cards. It makes me so happy! It's the little things, right?

Christmas in Nashville is really something, complete with advanced-placement caroling. As kids, we would often go out caroling to raise money for a worthy cause. When we were younger, our parents went with us. When we were older, groups of friends would go out on their own, caroling up Belle Meade Boulevard and all the surrounding neighborhoods.

Since moving to Los Angeles, I've organized my own caroling parties. One year, I didn't do the party, and people were so upset that I was forced to start it back up. People told me they missed it, because it's very rare in Los Angeles to have a moment when people take time to remember traditional carols.

Here's how my party goes: We have a yummy dinner of ham and biscuits, always. Just ham and biscuits. Simple. Holidays always just say ham to me. There's nothing like a honey-baked ham. Once everyone's had some ham and biscuits and some drinks, we gather around the piano and start singing carols.

I think it's so fun when someone's playing the piano. There's something really joyful about it. And now that I've been in Hollywood awhile, I've learned that great piano players are usually up for playing the piano at the party. I took piano lessons for five years, but it totally eluded me. I was just butterfingers. So it took me a while to believe

my piano-playing friends when they offered to play. After all, if you're an actor or a comedian, you're not usually happy when somebody asks you to say your famous line from the famous movie you were in or to crack a joke on the spot. But musicians? Turns out they are often literally sitting on their hands waiting until someone asks them to play. I thought, "Oh, they'll want to relax." Nope. They relax once they're sitting on that piano bench, banging out "Hark! The Herald Angels Sing" or "Have Yourself a Merry Little Christmas."

Now, a lot of people don't know the words to even the most common carols. Between you and me, I find this befuddling. How do you make it to adulthood without ever picking up at least one verse of "Joy to the World"? Were you raised in a bunker? In case you were, in fact, raised in a cave, I have lyrics books made up for anyone who needs them. We sing and sing until we're hoarse. It's very cathartic to sing for a couple of hours at the top of your lungs surrounded by all your friends.

It's a beautiful, joyful time of harmony until the inevitable annual argument about who gets to sing the "FIVE GOL-DEN RINGS" solo in "The Twelve Days of Christmas." Every year, several guests lobby hard for the privilege of singing "FIVE GOL-DEN RINGS." All my friends know that it's a very big deal if you get that solo, a clear sign that you are an exceptional singer and one who has waged a successful campaign to be chosen. Our best soloist was definitely Neil Patrick Harris. His was by far the best Five Golden Rings of all time. He should really think about doing a Christmas album. Kate Hudson is a close second—she sings like the best bluesy lounge singer in the land.

But of course the most special part of the holiday is seeing the kids' faces on Christmas morning. We do stockings on Christmas Eve, and Santa comes at night. I always make the same two things for breakfast: breakfast casserole (sausage and white bread and eggs, baked with cheese on top) and an applesauce cake, which is like a coffee cake. I usually prep it the night before.

The kids wake up insanely early. My one rule is that Mom has to have one cup of coffee and put on her robe before we go downstairs. One year our Christmas started at four a.m. and was over by five thirty. It was ridiculous. Once all the presents had been opened, we all went back to bed. It gave new meaning to the phrase "too soon."

Applesauce Cake

FOR THE CAKE

1 cup (2 sticks) butter, softened

2 cups sugar

3 cups applesauce

3 cups all-purpose flour

1 teaspoon cinnamon

1 teaspoon nutmeg

1¾ teaspoons baking soda

½ teaspoon salt

1 cup golden raisins

1 cup chopped pecans

1 teaspoon vanilla extract

FOR THE BROWN SUGAR ICING

2 cups packed light brown sugar

⅓ cup heavy cream

4 tablespoons (½ stick) butter

1 teaspoon vanilla extract

1 cup sifted confectioner's sugar

½ teaspoon salt

This old-fashioned cake is very easy to mix up, and it tastes even better when it's a day or two old. It goes great with coffee, and nothing says "Happy holidays!" like cake for breakfast.

Preheat the oven to 325°F.

TO MAKE THE CAKE

1. Grease and flour a 9-inch bundt or tube pan. In a mixing bowl, cream together the butter and sugar until light and fluffy. Mix in the applesauce on a low speed. The butter mixture will separate a little from the applesauce, so don't worry that they don't mix together completely. In a separate bowl, sift together the flour, cinnamon, nutmeg, baking soda, and salt. Remove ¼ cup of the flour mixture and dredge the raisins and pecans in it. Fold the remaining flour mixture slowly into the applesauce mixture until just combined. Add the raisin and pecan mixture along with the vanilla extract and stir together by hand.

2. Pour into the prepared pan and bake for 1½ hours or until a toothpick inserted into the center part of the cake comes out clean. Let cool slightly and remove the cake from the pan, allowing it to cool completely.

TO MAKE THE BROWN SUGAR ICING

In a small saucepan, combine the brown sugar, cream, and butter. Over medium heat, bring the mixture to a boil, stirring occasionally until smooth. Remove from the heat and stir in the vanilla extract, confectioner's sugar,

and salt until smooth. Very quickly pour the icing over the cake, allowing it to spread and drip down the sides to set. The icing sets up very quickly, so it looks best when it is allowed to flow naturally.

Easter

Would you believe that as much as I love Christmas, it's not even my favorite holiday? My favorite holiday is Easter. Easter is a big deal in the South. We get real competitive with our egg decorating, and there are a million Easter egg hunts all over Nashville. We would do one at home when we woke up, then one at church, then one at a botanical garden. They weren't easy, either. The grassy hill behind the church where our Sunday school teachers hid eggs was slick as glass if you were wearing brand-new Easter shoes, so many a child would wipe out, grass-staining the heck out of their frilly dresses and seersucker suits. Still: we got *really good* at finding Easter eggs, y'all.

My mother helped the Easter bunny by making our Easter baskets special. She went out of her way to find some treasure from the local sweet shop—one little bag of the most delicious candies on Earth or a single exquisite Belgian chocolate bunny—to put in a basket she embellished with a satin ribbon or pretty spring flowers. My friends often had mountains of drugstore candy that at the time I thought looked pretty fantastic, but now I think that with her baskets my mother was teaching me a valuable lesson about quality over quantity. She changed the way I thought about food: the more time that's taken and the more care that's put into something, the better it is.

I also love Easter because it's about new beginnings. It drives home how time is passing and also how lucky we are to be seeing another spring. Everything about the celebration reminds us that we are blessed to be in a beautiful environment. We've made it through

How to Force Bulbs

Every winter, I buy some paperwhite or tulip bulbs. You can buy them already started in dirt or in water, or you can plant them yourself—either in soil or water. They don't like dirt that's too moist, so if you put them in a pretty, decorative container without drainage on the bottom, you should put down some gravel or lava rocks on the bottom, then soil over that. And the bulbs don't like to be fully buried. Let them stick out halfway. Partial sunlight is plenty. Watch them grow for a couple of weeks and then bloom. Voilà, spring indoors!

the cold, dark winter. Now the daffodils are blossoming and the trees are budding. Tulips were always a big thing in my family. My dad took great pride in planting tulip bulbs every winter so they would pop up at Easter time—gorgeous red and yellow in a perfect circle in our flower bed.

My girlfriend Heather and I always enjoy forcing bulbs, usually paperwhites. They're a reminder that something beautiful can come out of dormancy, just like the world around you is waking up to spring. It always reminds me of my dad and his prized flower bed.

easter lunch

Easter Rolls

Baked Ham

Mama's Biscuits

Sweet Potato Casserole with
Candied Pecan Crust

Asparagus with Mock Hollandaise Sauce

Mile-High Lemon Meringue Pie

Easter Rolls

¼ cup dark brown sugar

¼ cup light corn syrup

4 tablespoons butter

Dash salt

½ cup coarsely chopped toasted pecans

12 frozen Parker House–style rolls (from a 25-oz. package)

1. Combine the sugar, corn syrup, butter, and salt in a small saucepan and bring to a simmer over medium-low heat; cook, stirring constantly, for 1 minute. Remove from heat and stir in the pecans.

2. Divide the pecan-syrup mixture evenly among the cups of a 12-cup muffin pan (about 1 tablespoon in each cup). Place a frozen Parker House roll on top of the mixture in each cup. Cover with lightly greased plastic wrap and let sit at room temperature for 2½ to 3 hours, or until double in bulk.

3. Preheat the oven to 400°F.

4. Remove the plastic wrap and bake in the preheated oven for 12 to 15 minutes or until golden brown. Remove from the oven and let cool for 2 minutes. Turn the rolls out upside down on a serving platter and spoon the pecan mixture over the tops. Let cool slightly before serving.

Baked Ham

Baked Ham*

1 cup orange juice

1 cup maple syrup

1 cup honey

2 tablespoons stone-ground mustard

1 teaspoon ground cloves

1 teaspoon ground allspice

1 teaspoon ground cinnamon

2 tablespoons lemon zest

2 tablespoons orange zest

1 spiral-cut, cooked bone-in ham (about 6 to 8 pounds)

*OR PSSST... just buy a HoneyBaked Ham online. Their 10-pound hams serve about 20 people. I swear I don't work for them! I'm just being realistic. No one will know the difference. And if they do, they will be too happy and full to judge you. Glazes are messy and people are busy, especially around the holidays.

My grandmother loved to serve ham at Easter, sometimes covered in pineapple slices or basted in a brown-sugar and cola glaze. This recipe from my friend Annie Campbell is the perfect balance of sweet and salty, plus it's simple to make. I always serve a ham-and-biscuit buffet at my Christmas parties.

TO MAKE THE GLAZE

Combine the orange juice, maple syrup, honey, mustard, cloves, allspice, cinnamon, lemon zest, and orange zest in a small saucepan. Bring to a boil over high heat and then reduce to a simmer. Cook, stirring occasionally, until thick and syrupy, about 15 minutes. Strain the syrup through a fine mesh strainer and set aside until ready to use.

TO MAKE THE HAM

1. Preheat the oven to 250°F. Wrap the ham tightly with foil and place in a roasting pan. Transfer to the oven and cook until the ham reaches 120°F in the center, about 2½ hours. When done, remove it from the oven and unwrap. Increase the oven temperature to 400°F.

2. Brush the ham with one-third of the glaze. Return it to the oven and bake for 5 minutes. Brush the ham with another third of the glaze and bake until crisp and shiny, for about 10 minutes more. Remove from the oven and paint with the remaining glaze. Tent the ham with foil and let rest for 15 minutes before slicing and serving.

3. Serve the ham on a platter alongside assorted mustards and dinner rolls.

Mama's Biscuits

2 cups flour

2 teaspoons baking powder

¼ teaspoon baking soda

¼ teaspoon salt

4 tablespoons vegetable shortening

⅔ or ¾ cup buttermilk

1. Preheat the oven to 450°F.

2. Combine the flour, baking powder, baking soda, and salt; mix well. Cut in the shortening with a pastry blender until the mixture resembles coarse meal.

3. Add the buttermilk, stirring just until the dry ingredients are moistened. Turn the dough out onto a floured surface; knead 3 or 4 times.

4. Roll the dough to ½-inch thickness; cut with a 2½-inch biscuit cutter. Place the biscuits on a greased baking sheet. Bake for 10 minutes, or until the tops are golden.

An Easter Playlist

"APRIL IN PARIS"	"A-TISKET, A-TASKET"	"HEY BOY! HEY GIRL!"
BILLIE HOLIDAY	ELLA FITZGERALD	LOUIS PRIMA AND KEELY SMITH
"SPRING CAN REALLY HANG YOU UP THE MOST"	"LA VIE EN ROSE"	"I'VE GOT THE WORLD ON A STRING"
ELLA FITZGERALD	ÉDITH PIAF	ANITA O'DAY
"IT'S A GOOD DAY"	"LIMEHOUSE BLUES"	"SALT PEANUTS"
PEGGY LEE	DJANGO REINHARDT	DIZZY GILLESPIE

Biscuit-Making Tips

Biscuits are such a staple in the South that making them can be intimidating until you get the hang of it. Here are a few secrets that might help.

- Start with cold butter cut into small chunks. You can cut the butter and then hold it in the freezer while you get your other ingredients together.

- Mix all the dry ingredients together well before you start.

- Use a pastry cutter to blend the butter into the flour; this keeps the butter cold. You can use your hands if you have to, but work quickly because the heat from your hands will start to heat up the butter.

- Blend the butter into the flour until the mixture resembles coarse oatmeal or pea-sized clumps. This technique creates little pockets of butter spread throughout the dough, resulting in a buttery, flaky texture in each biscuit as the butter melts into the dough.

- After milk or buttermilk is added, don't knead the dough. Just mix it with your hands until the milk is incorporated and the dough resembles a loose, shaggy blob. Once you put the dough out on the floured surface, it will start to come together into a rollable dough.

- Keep a little measuring cup or pile of extra flour near your rolling surface so that you can easily grab a little more flour to sprinkle on if the dough starts to stick.

- Sprinkle some flour onto a rolling surface and pat some flour onto your hands when you are ready to turn out the dough onto the surface. Rub the rolling pin with a bit of flour, too.

- Roll out the first pass to about an inch thick, then fold the dough over onto itself and roll out again. The first couple of passes will need a little more flour patted onto the dough and the rolling pin. Roll out again, this time to about ½ inch thick. Fold the dough over itself in half and then again into fourths—this is what creates layers in a biscuit!

- Roll one last time, until the dough is about ½ inch thick. Press a biscuit cutter or even the open end of a juice glass into some flour and then cut out biscuits as close to the edges and each other as possible.

- VERY IMPORTANT! When cutting out the biscuits, do not twist the cutter. Press straight down and back up. Twisting the cutter creates a seal around the edges of the dough, resulting in biscuits that cannot raise up as high when baking.

- You can roll out the dough that remains after cutting the first batch, but try not to knead the dough too vigorously. The more you work the dough, the tougher the biscuits will be.

- Place the biscuits on an ungreased baking sheet right up next to the edge of the sheet and right next to each other with their sides touching. This helps them rise rather than spread out, creating taller, flakier biscuits.

- Use the dough left from the second round of cutting to roll out into a "snake," and then press the snake to the edges of the biscuits that are on the outside of the rows of cut biscuits. Depending on the size of your baking sheet and how much dough there is, it is very likely that your biscuits will not fill the pan all the way. Lining the outer biscuits with the snake helps those biscuits rise up tall. Plus, when the pan comes out of the oven, it's fun to watch the kids fight over who gets to eat the biscuit snake. (See page 77 for photo.)

- Halfway through the baking process, spin the baking sheet 180 degrees. All ovens are different, and sometimes the biscuits don't rise evenly because of the pan's proximity to the sides of the oven. Spinning the tray halfway through helps the biscuits rise and bake more evenly.

- Once you remove the biscuits from the oven, immediately brush them with melted butter. This creates a beautiful sheen and is, of course, delicious.

Sweet Potato Casserole with Candied Pecan Crust

8 medium sweet potatoes (about 3½ pounds), peeled

⅓ cup Grade B maple syrup

1½ teaspoons salt

1 teaspoon vanilla extract

1 teaspoon cinnamon

⅓ cup heavy cream

1 cup mini marshmallows (optional)

½ cup all-purpose flour

½ cup packed dark brown sugar

¼ teaspoon kosher salt

Freshly grated nutmeg

4 tablespoons cold butter, cut into small cubes

½ cup toasted pecan pieces

1. Preheat the oven to 375°F. Lightly grease an 11-by-7-inch baking dish.

2. Slice the potatoes and place in a Dutch oven. Fill the pan with water to just cover the slices. Bring to a boil over high heat. Reduce heat to low, cover, and simmer until tender, about 15 minutes. Drain and transfer to a large bowl.

3. Add the maple syrup, salt, vanilla extract, cinnamon, and cream to the hot potatoes. Mash with a potato masher or beat with a hand mixer until smooth. Transfer the puree to the prepared baking dish. Top evenly with mini marshmallows, if desired.

4. To prepare the crust, combine the flour, sugar, salt, and a few gratings of nutmeg in a bowl. Cut the butter cubes into the mixture using two knives or a pastry blender until it resembles coarse meal. Stir in the pecan pieces and sprinkle over the top of the casserole. Cover with foil and bake for 15 minutes. Uncover and continue baking for 20 to 25 minutes, or until the top is caramelized and fragrant.

Asparagus with Mock Hollandaise Sauce

2 bunches thick
asparagus spears,
trimmed

2 tablespoons
kosher salt

**MOCK HOLLANDAISE
SAUCE**

½ stick butter

Freshly grated zest
of 1 lemon

1 cup good mayonnaise,
such as Hellman's or
Best Foods

1 teaspoon Dijon mustard

Freshly squeezed juice
of 1 lemon

¼ teaspoon salt

Pinch of cayenne pepper

Fresh asparagus is a sure sign of spring. Hollandaise is a perfect pairing that some people avoid making because it can separate and it's hard to keep if you don't use it right away. Dorothea handed down to me this easy recipe for Mock Hollandaise Sauce made with store-bought mayonnaise. It might be cheating a bit, but it's so tasty I doubt you'll hear any complaints.

Fill a large sauté pan or asparagus steamer with water and bring to a boil over high heat. Add the asparagus and salt and cook for 6 minutes. Remove the pan from the heat and drain the asparagus. Immediately transfer the spears to a bowl of ice water to shock them and lock in the bright green color. When cool, drain again.

TO MAKE THE MOCK HOLLANDAISE SAUCE

1. Melt the butter and add the lemon zest. Set aside. In a food processor or blender, blend the mayonnaise, Dijon mustard, lemon juice, salt, and cayenne pepper. Slowly drizzle in the melted butter through the feed tube a little at a time to incorporate. Taste and adjust seasoning.

2. The asparagus may be served at room temperature or reheated in the sauté pan or an asparagus steamer filled with simmering water for 1 minute. Drain and arrange on a warm serving platter. Serve with the sauce.

Mile-High Lemon Meringue Pie

One 9-inch prebaked
pie shell

FOR THE FILLING

6 large eggs

2 large egg yolks

2 cups sugar

Finely grated zest of
4 lemons (about
2 tablespoons)

Freshly squeezed juice of
4 lemons (¾ cup)

1 cup softened butter

FOR THE MERINGUE

6 large egg whites

⅛ teaspoon salt

¼ teaspoon cream
of tartar

6 tablespoons
powdered sugar

Preheat the oven to 300°F.

TO MAKE THE FILLING

Whisk together the eggs, egg yolks, and sugar in a small saucepan. Cook over medium-low heat for 7 to 8 minutes, whisking constantly, until the mixture thickens and forms a custard (like a thick eggnog) and reaches 165°F. Remove from heat and mix in the lemon zest, lemon juice, and butter; let cool while making the meringue.

TO MAKE THE MERINGUE

1. Whisk the egg whites in a bowl with a mixer or by hand until frothy. Add the salt and cream of tartar and beat until stiff but not dry. Beat in the powdered sugar ½ tablespoon at a time until incorporated. Continue beating until the meringue is glossy and holds its shape well.

2. Pour the lemon custard into the pie shell. Spoon the meringue on top of the filled pie and spread gently into waves with a spatula to the edges of the crust. Bake in the preheated oven for 15 minutes. Turn off the oven and let the pie cool for 45 minutes with the oven door closed. Remove to a wire rack and let cool to room temperature before serving.

Halloween

Hayrides and pumpkin patches, mazes and quilts . . . I love this time of year. And because, guys . . . I'm an actor! I love a costume that involves full makeup and a wig—a complete transformation. One time when Deacon was only one and Ava was five, we all got dressed up to go to a neighborhood Halloween party. I went as Sally from *The Nightmare Before Christmas*. Well, we arrived at the party and . . . I was the only grown-up in a costume! That's right: I had to sip cocktails at this party of fifty adults while I was in a full face of rag-doll makeup and a yarn wig. Embarrassing, yes, but I believe it speaks volumes about my commitment to holidays.

On this theme: last Halloween, I had a bunch of hay bales plus forty-seven pumpkins in the yard outside my house. I kind of went overboard, pumpkin-wise—and it took me a while to figure out what to do with them after Thanksgiving (there's only so much pumpkin bread a family can eat), but we had a lot of fun pretending we lived in the middle of a pumpkin patch.

Fourth of July

You have to go somewhere and sit on a grassy lawn and watch fireworks—somewhere, anywhere. And you have to drink American beer on the Fourth of July. You have to. It's a rule. And eat hot dogs. Even if you don't like them. No arguing. You have to. Salads tomorrow. But on the Fourth, it's all macaroni and cheese, hot dogs and hamburgers, and American beer. That's it. God bless America.

New Year's Eve
and New Year's Day

To start the year off right, it's customary in the South to eat a big, lucky meal of Hoppin' John (black-eyed peas and rice), collards, and corn bread (or simple hoe cakes, like the ones on page 271). Southern superstition has it that eating collards on New Year's means you'll make plenty of money in the new year. Speaking of rich: this dish is far from light. After this meal, expect everyone to need a nap. New Year's Day is a great day for open houses, too. Friends drop by to eat these treats, drink plenty of beer and Bloody Marys as a "hair of the dog" hangover cure, and wish one another good fortune for the coming year. If you're enjoying a warm southern winter, you can play a game of horseshoes out in the yard for extra good luck.

Hoppin' John

4 to 6 slices thick-cut bacon, chopped roughly

1 cup chopped celery

1 cup chopped onions

1 cup chopped green pepper

3 garlic cloves, minced

1 teaspoon salt

½ teaspoon freshly ground black pepper

8 cups chicken broth

4 cups fresh, frozen, or soaked dried black-eyed peas

1½ cups basmati or long-grain rice

Chopped scallions for garnish

Every southerner has a favorite recipe for this classic dish. Some may insist that you use only fresh peas. In my kitchen, it's fine to use fresh, dried, or frozen. Just be sure if you are using dried beans to soak them overnight or use the "quick soak" method on the package.

1. In a Dutch oven or large saucepot, cook the bacon over medium heat, stirring occasionally, until it has rendered some of its fat and is just beginning to get crispy. Add the celery, onions, and green pepper and cook until the vegetables begin to get soft. Add the garlic and cook for 1 minute more. Sprinkle with salt and pepper and add the chicken broth and peas. Increase the heat to medium-high and bring to a boil. Reduce the heat to low and simmer for about 30 minutes, or until the peas are tender but not falling apart.

2. Strain the pea mixture, reserving the cooking liquid; return the pea mixture to the pot along with about 1 cup of the cooking liquid, and keep warm over very low heat. In a medium saucepan, combine the rice and 2 cups of the reserved cooking liquid (add water if there is not enough to make 2 cups) and bring to a boil. Reduce the heat to low and cover with a tight-fitting lid. Cook for about 15 minutes without lifting the lid. Check the rice to see if all of the liquid has been absorbed. If not, keep it on the heat for a few minutes more, and when done, fluff it with a fork. Serve the peas and rice together on a plate with collard greens (see folllowing) and sprinkle with fresh scallions.

Braised Collard Greens in Smoky Ham Hock Broth

SMOKY HAM HOCK BROTH

2 quarts chicken or vegetable stock

1 large onion, peeled and quartered

4 garlic cloves, peeled and smashed

1 dried red pepper

1 smoked ham hock

COLLARD GREENS

2 bunches (2 pounds) collard greens

2 tablespoons olive oil

1 Vidalia or other sweet onion, chopped

2 cloves garlic, minced

2 teaspoons salt

¼ teaspoon sugar

1 teaspoon freshly ground black pepper

Smoky Ham Hock Broth (see above)

Pepper vinegar (e.g., Trappey's pepper vinegar)

Hot sauce

Today raw kale and quickly sautéed collards may be all the rage, but when I was growing up, my grandma's greens simmered for hours on the stove. You could smell that collards were on the menu before you even got to the front door. Serve these with hot sauce and pepper vinegar.

TO MAKE THE BROTH

Put all the ingredients into a large saucepot and bring to a boil over high heat. Reduce to a simmer and cook for 1 to 1½ hours. Pour the broth through a strainer; reserve the red pepper pod and the ham hock but throw out the rest of what is left in the strainer. On a cutting board, remove the meat from the hock bone and return it to the pot. Slice the reserved pepper pod and return it to the strained broth. Keep the broth on a low simmer until you are ready to cook the collard greens.

NOTE: You can make the broth a day or two ahead and keep in the refrigerator until you are ready to use it—just heat it up in a pot before cooking the collards.

TO MAKE THE COLLARD GREENS

1. Wash the collard greens by soaking them in a sink filled with water, allowing any gritty sand or soil to sink

Continued...

to the bottom. Remove the thick stems from the leaves by holding each stem in one hand and pinching the leaf around the stem at the widest bottom part with your other hand. Pull the leaf and stem away from each other in one sweeping move. Remove any large leafy parts that remain. In batches, stack a handful of the leaves and roll them up into a cigar shape. Then slice crossways with a large knife to create about ¼-inch-wide ribbons. Place the ribbons in a bowl and set aside—do not spin or dry the leaves.

2. In a large stockpot, heat the olive oil over medium–high heat. Saute the onions for a minute or two, until they begin to soften. Add the garlic and salt and sauté for another minute. Put handfuls of the collard ribbons into the oil and onion mixture (you may have to do this in batches if your pot fills up—as the leaves cook, they will wilt to a much smaller size). Wilt the greens by turning them over with tongs or a large wooden spoon or spatula to sauté them slightly and coat them with the oil. Sprinkle with the sugar as you sauté the greens (this will cut down on any bitterness and not really add sweetness to the greens), and the black pepper, then cover the greens with the smoky ham broth, including the ham hock meat and the sliced red pepper pod. Bring to a boil, then reduce the heat to low and simmer for 1 hour. Serve the collards with some of the "pot likker," the nutrient-rich broth that remains after cooking. Serve with the pepper vinegar and the hot sauce, allowing diners to sprinkle on as much as they like.

Corn Bread "Hoe Cakes"

2½ cups milk

2 tablespoons butter

1 cup all-purpose flour

2 cups cornmeal

2 teaspoons baking powder

1 teaspoon salt

2 eggs, slightly beaten

Vegetable oil for frying

Southern corn bread is a staple—cooked in a black iron skillet, it's hard to beat. But cornmeal pancakes or "hoe cakes" (also sometimes called johnnycakes) are crispy, delicious, and easy to make for a crowd. You can use a cornmeal mix and follow the directions on the package or just make this easy batter mixture.

1. In a small saucepan, combine the milk and butter and cook over medium heat until the butter melts.

2. In a large mixing bowl, stir together the flour, cornmeal, baking powder, and salt.

3. Stir the hot milk into the dry ingredients with a rubber spatula and then fold in the beaten eggs.

4. Cover the bottom of a cast-iron skillet or griddle with vegetable oil and heat over medium to medium-high heat.

5. Drop the batter onto the hot surface of the oil to make the hoe cakes into your desired size (just like pancakes). Cook until golden brown on both sides and transfer to a sheet pan set in a warm oven to hold until all the cakes are done. Serve with a relish such as chow-chow (a pickled southern relish) for a savory bite, or drizzle with butter and molasses or sorghum syrup for a sweet taste.

CHAPTER 16

The Beauty of Female Friendships

Loyalty is a real southern tradition, and so is protecting our women. These two virtues came together in a shameful incident I will call the Day of the Donut.

Here's what happened: My grandmother was getting on in years. She was probably eighty years old, but she was still mobile and enjoyed going to Kroger every morning to have her coffee and do a little grocery shopping. Some of her friends liked walking around the mall to get exercise, but she'd walk around Kroger. One morning she went to the local store as usual. Walking through the aisles, she came upon a sample tray on which there was a stack of donuts. She picked up a donut from the tray and began happily nibbling on it while she was moseying about.

Clothing and Bag Swaps

You know when you clean out your closet and you have all this stuff to get rid of? I believe in donating it to the local thrift store, but I like to use a couple of items as an excuse to throw a white elephant party. The way it works is this: You bring a gift—it could be ridiculous or wonderful—and put it on a table. Then you pick a number, say from 1 to 20 (based on the number of guests), and then whatever number you get is when it's your turn to pick a gift from the pile. You can keep the item or give it to someone else in exchange for the gift that he or she picked.

Or you can just do a more informal version where you bring clothes you don't want anymore, put them in the middle of the table, and take something else you do want. A handbag white elephant sale would be my idea of fun, because you kind of get sick of your bags after a while, and I always seem to covet my friends' purses. I also have friends who do this with books or their kids' books and clothes.

Whatever you're getting rid of, it's a fun way to clean your house, hang out with your girlfriends, and get some fun new things to mess up your house with again.

Well, the manager of Kroger decided that my grandmother had stolen the donut. Maybe it wasn't a sample tray after all? Unclear. What is clear is that he got into an intense argument with her over the supposedly illicit donut. And as you may have gathered by now, my grandmother was not to be argued with. She was a very fierce debater. So she gave that manager the what-for. And she arrived home outraged. And so, from that day forward, our entire family was not allowed to go to that particular Kroger. That's right; because of the disrespect that was shown toward my grandmother on that infamous day of the stolen donut, that Kroger is dead to us.

Bear in mind, I find this whole saga completely hysterical. It's absurd. Still, to this day, I will not go into that Kroger. I'll go into any other Kroger, just not that one, the donut one. This is about southern family loyalty. Decades shall pass, and the Witherspoons will never forget the twentieth-century donut insult!

So I think you know what I'm saying when I tell you I would boycott a Kroger for the women in my life. I've maintained friendships with a number of female friends since grammar school. They were incredibly important to me when I was growing up, and they still are. It means the world to me that when I go home to

Nashville, everybody who knew me before I had any success treats me the same as always.

Many of these old friends have lived in places such as Chicago, Dallas, and New York but have subsequently moved back to Nashville. I am really enjoying their stories of what it's like to return after fifteen years of living in other places. In many ways, Nashville is a different city from the one we grew up in. I see my old friends really enjoying the new attitudes, restaurants, entertainment, and culture. But there are some things that are still the same. For instance, they still put gigantic bows in their daughters' hair.

Houseguests

I love having houseguests. I think it's really fun. (Well, it's really fun for three days. Past that, I want to scream—something along the lines of "Take a hike!") I especially love hosting my family and close friends, because then the kids get good quality time with them. And it makes you closer to other people when you share a roof for a couple of days. Plus, they can babysit! We have friends we met on vacation who come and visit us, probably once a year. It's great. They're in the military, and they're interesting people who travel the world and tell us cool stories about faraway places.

Houseguests should always offer to help in whatever way they can. If you're a good cook, offer to cook. If you're a good cleaner, offer to clean. That offer is really appreciated even if your host won't let you do anything. When my brother comes and stays with me, I most definitely let him help out. (To be honest, I put him to work, because he's very handy.) Whenever he's here, he fixes everything in my house. He will fix my garbage disposal, or he'll check and make sure all my air-conditioning filters are clean. He'll ask about something like that, and I'll say, "Oh, my God. You're right. I need to do that!" And he'll say, "Don't worry, I already went to Home Depot, sister. I handled it." Gotta love a brother like that!

He'll spend half the time he's out here visiting fixing cars, fixing the house. My son follows him around like I followed my grandfather around, just absorbing every bit of wisdom. Deacon has become so handy thanks to his Uncle John's Home Depot tutorials.

No matter how long or short the visit, I find it's important to plan lots of activities to keep everyone busy and make sure everyone's out of the house for at least part of every day, so people aren't on top of one another and going crazy. And if you're a houseguest, it really helps to let your host know when you're arriving and when you're leaving. As a host, you need to know the beginning, middle, and end of a visit.

Another thing to keep in mind when hosting houseguests is an oldie but goodie: For goodness' sake, Don't Talk About Politics! People's politics don't always align, and conversations about news topics can turn a lovely brunch into a war zone. When family comes to my house for a visit, we try to keep it about family, levity, children, and enjoying the time with one another. It's so important to focus on what brings us together and not what could push us apart. The most important thing is that we're a family and we'll be together and care for each other, always.

And it's been fun to see our friendships evolve from when we were young to today, when we have careers and families. My feeling about friendship is quality over quantity. I have only a few really good friends, but they're wonderful people whom I trust implicitly. They're all interesting and have a lot going on in their lives. I'm a busy person, so I need to have busy friends who understand what it means to be busy. I don't have time for a friend who says, "Where have you *been*?"

Because where I've been is usually taking care of three children and a husband and a business and a career. My friends get that, and so when we are able to find time together, we can just pick back up as though no time has ever passed. Sometimes when I'm away making a movie, it can mean three months of radio silence. I miss my friends, and they miss me. But part of friendship at this age is getting used to those absences and appreciating it all the more when we're able to hang out.

When I'm in town, I make it a point to see my girlfriends at least once or twice a week. It's really important to me. We usually hike or do an exercise class. I find you exercise more if you have a buddy holding you to it. I'll show up for somebody else, but I won't always show up for myself alone. I have one best friend, Shannon, who I work out with. We hold each other to it. And having company makes it more fun. Although we usually talk so much that I don't think we burn many calories.

I love low-key evenings where our kids are running and playing around in the backyard and we just hang out and have a little dinner and catch up. Or a girlfriend and I do Sunday brunch at my house or hers. The kids swim or watch a movie, and we get to have a nice couple of hours to ourselves. Sometimes we even invite our husbands.

MENU

a brunch party

Brunch parties are generally more low-key
than formal dinners. I love throwing them for
a birthday, a baby or bridal shower, or just
a we-haven't-seen-each-other-in-ages
girls' get-together.

Cheese Wafers

Strawberry Fields Salad

Finger Sandwiches

Heather's Layer Cake

Cheese Wafers

3 cups freshly grated sharp cheddar cheese

1½ cups all-purpose flour, sifted

½ teaspoon baking powder

½ teaspoon kosher salt

1 stick butter, softened

⅛ to ¼ teaspoon cayenne pepper

Pecan halves

One southerner's cheese straw is another's cheese biscuit, wafer, or cracker. Whatever you call it, it's the quintessential southern pre-party nibble from brunch 'til supper. The great thing about this recipe, besides being crazy good, is that a single batch of dough makes plenty for a crowd plus extra to bundle up as favors for departing guests. Store any leftover cheese wafers in an airtight tin for cocktail-hour snacking. The dough freezes well, too.

1. Preheat the oven to 400°F.

2. Mix all of the ingredients except pecan halves in a mixing bowl to thoroughly combine.

3. Turn the dough out onto a lightly floured surface and roll out to about ¼-inch thickness. Cut the dough with a cutter into 2-inch rounds and arrange on two large baking sheets about 1 inch apart. Gather scraps into a ball and roll and cut one more time.

4. Arrange dough rounds on the baking sheets, about ½ inch apart, and press a pecan half gently into the center of each round. Bake in the preheated oven for 10 to 15 minutes, until they just begin to brown. Remove from the oven and cool completely on a wire rack.

Strawberry Fields Salad

FOR THE SALAD

1 (7 oz.) package baby spinach

1 quart strawberries, washed

½ cup crumbled blue cheese

¼ cup chopped toasted pecans

FOR THE SESAME VINAIGRETTE DRESSING

⅓ cup rice vinegar

1 tablespoon soy sauce

2 tablespoons toasted sesame oil

2 tablespoons vegetable oil

2 tablespoons toasted sesame seeds

¼ cup water

The Nashville bakery-café Bread & Company serves one of my all-time favorite salads. It's called "Strawberry Fields." When I can't get there to have the real deal, I make a version of it with most of the same ingredients, winging the proportions. Go get theirs if you can, but if you can't, here's what you need to do to approximate it at home.

TO MAKE THE SALAD

1. Fill a large bowl with the spinach.

2. Dice the strawberries and add them to the bowl.

3. Sprinkle in the blue cheese.

4. Add a handful of chopped pecans.

5. Mix up and serve with sesame vinaigrette.

TO MAKE THE DRESSING

Whisk all of the ingredients together and serve immediately or store up to 1 month in the refrigerator.

Finger Sandwiches

My grandmother Dorothea's cookbook proclaims, "Delicacy is the operative word" when it comes to tea sandwiches. It tells us to use "fine-grained, moist, well-flavored bread that can be spread with softened sweet butter without tearing." This bread must be sliced wafer-thin. You can keep it moist between damp paper towels. But caution! "Be generous with fillings but not so that the sandwiches ooze." Got that? Southern-lady ghosts will haunt you if there's oozing.

Below are some options for sandwich fillings. I like to make a bunch of each kind and set them in piles with a note about which is which. You can get creative with all kinds of meats and vegetables and cheeses, but these are the most satisfying and most traditional options, in my grandmother's opinion!

CUCUMBER: Peel and deseed the cucumber, slice it thinly, then soak it in water with salt and sugar for an hour. Drain the slices and put on buttered bread, season with salt and pepper, and cut into rectangles.

WATERCRESS: No preparation is needed. Just put the cress (American—not English—watercress, the book insists) onto buttered bread. Cut into triangles. Make sure they're kept cool.

TOMATO: Peel, seed, thin-slice, and salt tomatoes. Put on buttered white or whole wheat bread.

CHICKEN: This is a good use for leftover white meat. Put between slices of white or whole wheat bread with plenty of mayo, salt, and pepper.

HAM: Put thin-sliced ham on bread that has butter on one side, mayo and mustard on the other.

PIMENTO CHEESE: Pimento cheese is not for everybody, but I find it particularly delicious on Ritz crackers. And it's surprisingly simple to make. You just mix a block of sharp cheddar, grated, with a couple of ounces each of cream cheese and mayonnaise, and a half or so little jar of pimento, diced, plus salt and pepper to taste.

Heather's Layer Cake

FOR THE CAKE

6 room-temperature large eggs, separated

3¼ cups sugar, divided

2 sticks unsalted butter, softened

2 teaspoons vanilla extract

1 teaspoon coconut extract

1½ teaspoons baking soda

¾ cup buttermilk

¾ cup canned coconut milk

2 teaspoons salt

4 cups sifted cake flour

FOR THE WHIPPED CREAM FROSTING

4 cups heavy cream

⅓ cup plus 2 tablespoons granulated sugar

½ teaspoon vanilla extract

2 teaspoons coconut extract

Fresh flower blossoms for garnish

For my bridal and baby showers, my friend Heather made this pretty white cake with the lightest cake layers sandwiching airy clouds of whipped cream, topped with fresh flower blossoms. It's so delicate that it's best eaten the day it's made.

Preheat the oven to 325°F. Grease and flour two round 3-by-10-inch cake pans.

TO MAKE THE CAKE

1. Using an electric mixer, beat the egg whites in a mixing bowl until soft peaks form. Slowly beat in ¼ cup of the sugar until the mixture thickens to stiff, glossy peaks. Set aside.

2. In a separate bowl, cream the butter with the remaining 3 cups of sugar. Add the vanilla and coconut extracts, and, one at a time, add the egg yolks, beating after each addition until blended.

3. In another bowl, stir the baking soda into the buttermilk and coconut milk and set aside.

4. Sift together the salt and cake flour and, alternating with the milks, add each to the butter mixture. Fold the egg whites into the batter. Divide the batter between the prepared pans.

5. Bake for 45 minutes or 1 hour, until a toothpick inserted in the center of each cake comes out clean. Run a knife around the edge of each cake and let the cakes cool in the pans on a wire rack for 20 minutes. Invert the cakes on the rack and remove the pans. Let the cakes continue to cool completely before frosting.

6. Slice each cake horizontally into two layers with a serrated knife to make four layers. Arrange the first layer on a cake stand and top with 2 cups of the frosting, using an offset spatula to spread the frosting just to the cake edges. Repeat with the next 2 layers. For the final layer, spread the remaining frosting on top of the cake. Arrange fresh flower blossoms artfully on the top of the cake.

TO MAKE THE FROSTING

Chill a mixing bowl and the beaters of the mixer in the freezer for 5 minutes. Beat the cream on medium-high speed until it begins to thicken. Reduce the speed to medium and slowly beat in the sugar until soft peaks form. Add the vanilla and coconut extracts and beat until the whipped cream holds stiff peaks.

Tip : Use edible blossoms if you wish; otherwise, be sure to tell your guests that they are just for show.

CHAPTER 17

Do-Gooding

One thing the South does really well is community. I think it's because we link charity and giving back with two other things we do well: cooking and entertaining. A fund raiser is a great reason to get dressed up, go out with friends, and enjoy good food. Giving back is woven into the fabric of life.

At the high school that my dad, my uncle, and my brother attended, they have a spaghetti potluck dinner every November. All the families get together and cook pasta. Either you bring the spaghetti or you bring the corn bread or you bring the spaghetti sauce or the sides. It's the hugest potluck you've ever seen, and it's all a big benefit for the school. It's something we all looked forward to.

My grandfather Jimmy taught me so much about belonging to charity organizations and taking care of other people. He personally funded scholarships for nurses. He gave his time to the Boys & Girls Clubs of America and served in Big Brothers Big Sisters of America, too. He participated in pretty much every community group there was, from the American Legion to March of Dimes.

At Christmastime, he would have me and my brother help him deliver food and toys to families that were struggling. My grandfather had an innate need to do good for others all the time. He taught me that if you come across someone in need, you get out your wallet, reach in, pull out whatever's there, and give it to the person who needs it more than you. He always lived by the motto that charity starts at home, in your neighborhood. On a regular basis, he would go into his garden and bag up great bunches of vegetables for the local food bank.

I've tried to follow his example. When I launched Draper James, I insisted that we give back to the community. We partnered with a group called Girls, Inc. to create after-school programs for girls in every area where there's a Draper James store. Girls, Inc. is one of the United States' oldest charities. Its members help girls learn basic, essential skills, such as social media best practices and financial literacy. In my experience, girls don't talk enough about money. They should! It's a huge part of your life. You need to know how to manage your money and feel empowered by it, not scared of it. Another thing that I really want my kids, as well as the after-school girls, to learn is that it's so important to reach out when you need help and to be there to help others when you're strong.

If you live in a southern community and your family is going through an important life event, whether a birth or death or move, your neighbors are liable to show up on your doorstep offering warm words and usually something in a Pyrex dish. I think it means so much when people have a brand-new baby and you go to their house to hold the baby for a little while so they can shower or nap and then you leave them something like a bottle of wine and a bunch of great takeout and a present. Similarly, when your friends move to a new house, it means so much to show up and give them something to help them get settled. Or when they're going through a transition or a divorce or a loss, you have to go. You have to be there for them however you can.

My husband's father died when my husband was thirty-nine, so I ask him for advice whenever I'm not sure how to handle a friend's loss. I always talk to him about how to write condolence letters and whether or not to call the person's family.

Jim always says, "Just make the call. Even if you don't know what to say, just pick up the phone and make the call."

Whenever I hear that someone's died, I always think about him saying that, and I just dial.

It's an excellent rule of thumb: Just write the letter. Do it promptly. Say something about the person that was meaningful to you, something specific that would be a nice memory for the recipient.

Yes, it's so hard to know what to say. I once read a book about how to have difficult conversations, and the most important thing that I learned from it was that you don't have to say something extremely profound or absolutely perfect. The important thing is that you show you care. You can admit that you really don't know what to write. That's fine. You are showing that you care, and that's what's important.

Also, and this is particular to me, I never send flowers. I don't send flowers because they wilt, and they remind you of loss and sadness. Instead, I take food, because it's practical. You can eat it, and then it's gone. At such times, there are always people around whom the family have to feed. I usually take a casserole, lasagna, or macaroni and cheese, all of which you can freeze to use later. Best of all is my chicken pot pie casserole, which is just a big hug. You can make this the traditional way, with bread crumbs on top, or sometimes I use frozen puff pastry topping to give it something extra.

Reese's Chicken Pot Pie Casserole

2 eggs

2 cups frozen shredded hash browns

2 teaspoons salt, divided

2 teaspoons freshly ground black pepper, divided

1 tablespoon vegetable or olive oil

1 cup onion, chopped

1 cup carrots, diced

1 cup celery, diced

1 cup frozen peas

1 cup cooked chicken, diced

1 (10.75 oz.) can cream of mushroom soup

1 sheet frozen puff pastry

1. Preheat the oven to 400°F.

2. Spray a 9-inch square casserole dish with cooking oil or rub with softened butter. In a mixing bowl, beat the eggs and add the frozen shredded hash browns and 1 teaspoon of the salt and pepper, tossing to coat the potatoes with egg. Press the hash brown mixture into the bottom of the prepared dish and bake for 15 minutes.

3. In a skillet, heat the oil over medium-high heat and sauté the onions, carrots, and celery for about 3 minutes until they just begin to soften. Remove from heat and stir in the frozen peas.

4. In a large mixing bowl, combine the chicken, vegetables, remaining teaspoon of salt and pepper, and cream of mushroom soup. Pour some water (about ¼ cup) into the empty soup can and swirl to get any remaining soup out, and pour the water into the chicken and vegetable mixture. Mix together well and pour on top of the cooked hash browns.

5. Unfold the puff pastry sheet and place over the top of the casserole. Bake about 35 minutes, until the casserole is bubbly and the top becomes puffy and brown.

The New South

So let's all move to the South! Today there are more building cranes in Nashville, Tennessee, than in New York City. All over town, you can see constant construction, new restaurants opening, and great people moving in. It's no surprise, really. Even with all the new buildings, there's a lot of wide-open green space for kids and dogs. And the city epitomizes southern hospitality.

What I love most about my part of the South today, though, is that although it retains its old glamour, it's becoming ever more open and creative and welcoming to all. There's a glorious mix of tradition and progress. Young people born in the South are going off to other parts of the country for college and then returning to Nashville with new ideas about food, about art, about culture, and helping the South grow into a new, thriving community of forward thinkers. You still have Steeplechase and hot rollers. But now you also have Bikram yoga, organic farming, and tech start-ups. And people are much more aware of one another and the big world they're a part of.

And, if you can believe it, the music just keeps getting better. Rock stars, indie bands, pop stars, and country artists continue to make Nashville the number one city in the country for music lovers. More than ever, there's an openness about collaboration—an artists' culture. Nashville has changed because the world is evolving. Music is about sharing the joy of life with the world—the whole world.

You know I'm a southern girl because fans come up to me and say things like "I know just from hearing you talk that we'd be best friends!"

They're probably right! For me, there are no strangers. Like my mom, these days I can talk to anyone about anything for hours.

But as I think you've seen in this book, the South is about more than manners and hosting. It's also about rowdy backyard parties and the kids running around the lawn in their pajamas on Easter morning and a bunch of gals drinking wine on the porch, laughing loudly and telling secrets. The South is about hospitality in the oldest sense. People there really enjoy meeting new people and making them feel at home, making them feel seen and heard and appreciated. The South is about enjoying this one life you've got.

Fortunately, that feeling is something you can re-create anywhere. I hope that everything in this book is something you can use, no matter the size of your home or budget. Wherever it is, I believe any home can be the coziest place on Earth.

If you think I sound proud of where I'm from, you're right. When it comes to the quality of our cooking and our parties, we southerners have trouble with modesty. We are proud of our heritage, our traditions, and—more than anything—whatever brings our families together around a table. I'm so honored that I could share a little piece of my southern background, my grandmother's recipes, and my most cherished family traditions with you! Y'all come back and visit sometime, ya hear?

Acknowledgments

Thank you to Trish Todd—a fellow Nashville girl who grew up with spiced tea, Steeplechase, and trips to Cheekwood—who had the idea for this book. You made me remember sweet memories long forgotten. And thanks to everyone at Touchstone, including Susan Moldow, Carolyn Reidy, Brian Belfiglio, Jessica Roth, Meredith Vilarello, Kelsey Manning, and Kaitlin Olson.

Thank you to Cait Hoyt for being my ultimate cheerleader and advocate. You helped me see the light when I almost gave up . . . many times! To Maha Dakhil, who never lets me drop the baton; and Meredith O'Sullivan, who makes sure I'm always connecting with the people who matter most: my fans.

And to my fans: How can I ever say thank you enough—for watching my movies, supporting my producing career, and now reading this book. I have the nicest, most positive fans in the world. If you even knew how much I think about you! I swear, I wake up thinking, *What do my fans want to see right now?* Please keep telling me. Whenever I meet you or hear from you, you give me strength to continue on this journey.

Thank you to Ada Calhoun—the master interpreter, the avid listener, the caretaker of my story. I will be forever grateful to you for learning how to understand my southern pride and my Tennessee accent.

Thank you to all the kind people who opened their homes to me for this book, including the Betherum, Stevens, and Caldwell families. I am so moved by your generosity and your southern hospitality.

A huge hug and thank-you to Hillary Franchi, who is a master producer—wearing every hat, keeping the ship on course, never complaining, and always encouraging me to see the big picture . . . You are one heck of a hardworking woman, without whom I could not be the woman I am today. It should also be noted that you are always down for a large glass of wine at the end of a hard day, and that is why we are friends.

To the dedicated soul who is the architect of my life, Rachel Bati, my oldest, dearest friend. There are not enough words to express my gratitude for the love and care you have brought to my personal life and my career for over twenty-five years. We have seen it *all*. I hope you know how much I love you.

Thank you to Beatrice, Adele, Miriam, Mayra, and Hilda for taking care of me and my family as though it were your own. You make the trains run on time, always find the soccer jersey, and get the chicken fingers onto the table. I will be forever grateful for the love you bring into my home.

Speaking of expertise, thank you to Paul Costello for finding the light, being my kindest collaborator, always seeing my vision, and raising the bar. Your artistry and second-to-none crew (hi, Alex, Zach, and Brent!) made this book possible.

Thanks to creative director Jenny Davis for her incredible vision and enthusiasm, and for making sure the angles were right and the sweet tea was sparkling. And the award for Bringing the Style goes to Colson Horton, for finding the beauty and the charm in every corner of the frame. Your love of thrift shopping finally paid off big-time!

I can't thank my beauty committee enough: Molly, Lona, Kelsey, Davey, Mai, Thuy, Derek. You brought the lashes, the lipstick, and the big hair like no others. I have the best team ever. Special shout-out to Tori, who hauled, steamed, and styled more clothes than a department store at Christmas. You are a superstar.

To food stylists Annie Campbell and Angie Mosier, who made all my grandma's recipes come alive. You reminded me that food is love—and that chili pie should be made more often.

To Heather, Jennie, Shannon, Ashley, Jenny, Mary Alice, Candace, Kate, and Laura, for being the sisters I never had. You have always been my true-blue besties, and nothing is better than sisterhood . . . well, maybe nachos. And margaritas. Thank you for always bringing the nachos, the margaritas, and the sisterhood.

To my nieces Abby James and Draper—thank you for missing school and dance recitals and Saturday activities to help with this book. Your sweet smiles light up my life.

To my brother, who called childhood friends and old stomping grounds to ask if we could visit again. You have always been my caretaker and my rock. Even if you fed me too many Hot Pockets as a kid, I forgive you. I love you to the moon and back, Brother John.

To my mom, who endured many photo sessions and interviews to make this book possible. Your joy and optimism have carried me through life. You are my greatest inspiration as a woman who lives every moment to the fullest, sees beauty and humor everywhere, and knows the importance of a good nap every day at four o'clock.

To my dad, for creating a living history for our family. Your love of our family history has always given me great pride in our humble beginnings. Thank you for always inspiring me to learn something new every day and to do more for others. A life of service is truly the best life.

To my grandmother Dorothea, for teaching me how to fry chicken and anything else that wasn't moving, to read great literature with passion, to dress for success, and to never wear workout clothes past ten in the morning.

To my granddad Jimmy, thank you for teaching me to love a backyard garden, to feed my neighbors and their dogs, and to always remember "to whom much is given, much is expected."

To my husband, Jim. I do not know how I got so lucky as to find a man like you. Your love and encouragement made this all possible. The way you hold my dreams in your heart has shown me that true love and real partnership are possible. On our first date, I told you the woman I wanted to be, and your endless support of me has helped me become that woman. As Pup said, "I take care of you, you take care of me, we take care of each other."

To Ava, Deacon, and Tennessee: Everything I do in this world is for you.

You are the most wonderful children a mother could hope for. I hope you always remember where you came from and never forget to pay everything forward. That's what my family taught me, and it has been the greatest guiding principle in my life. I hope you sing loudly at church, always dance at weddings, and whenever you hear "Sweet Home Alabama," I hope you smile.

Credits

CREATIVE DIRECTOR:
JENNIFER K. BEAL DAVIS

PRODUCER:
HILLARY FRANCHI

INTERIOR PHOTOGRAPHY:
PAUL COSTELLO AND ALEX DARSEY

FOOD STYLIST:
ANGIE MOSIER

PROP STYLING & SET DESIGN:
TAYLOR COLSON HORTON

ASSIST:
MIMI CORWIN, BRITTNEY FORRISTER,
KATHERINE STANFORD, AND ABBY DARBY

DERBY PARTY FOOD STYLIST:
ANNIE CAMPBELL

DERBY PARTY PROP STYLIST:
ZAC MITCHELL

MONOGRAMMING:
MARY NEAL

PHOTOS OF REESE ON
PAGES 5, 54 & BACK COVER:
COLIENA RENTMEESTER

PHOTOS ON PAGES 165 & 294:
ANGIE MOSIER

PHOTO ON PAGE 169:
COURTESY OF CHEEKWOOD

PHOTO ON PAGE 265:
FAITH ANN YOUNG

PHOTO ON PAGE 236:
MONICA HARVEY
OF SHOOTS AND GIGGLES
PHOTOGRAPHY

WALLPAPER BEHIND REESE ON BACK COVER:
CLARKE & CLARKE

"TREE OF LIFE" MURAL ON PAGE 5:
DESIGNED BY JAIMA BROWN EMMERT FOR
THE WALLPAPER COLLECTION WOODLANDS
RESOURCE BY DAISY BENNETT
(DAISYBENNETTDESIGNS.COM)

SILHOUETTES ON PAGE 217:
KARL JOHNSON / CUT ARTS

Recipe Index

Metric Conversion Charts

DRY INGREDIENTS	1 CUP EQUIVALENT (G)
Bell pepper (chopped)	175
Bread crumbs	120
Butter	225
Cake crumbs	75
Cereal	20
Cheddar (grated)	120
Chocolate chips	180
Coconut (shredded)	75
Condiments and thick sauces	220
Corn and peas	150
Cornmeal	170
Cream cheese	240
Cream (sour)	120
Cream (whipped)	60
Flour (all-purpose)	110
Flour (cake)	90

DRY INGREDIENTS	1 CUP EQUIVALENT (G)
Herbs and leaves	25
Honey and syrup	350
Marshmallows	50
Oats	80
Onion (chopped)	150
Parmesan (grated)	180
Pecans (chopped)	120
Raisins	150
Rice	210
Salt	240
Sugar (brown)	220
Sugar (confectioner's)	130
Sugar (granulated)	190
Tomatoes (chopped)	150
Walnuts (chopped)	115
Yogurt	250

LIQUID INGREDIENTS	1 CUP EQUIVALENT (ML)
General liquids (water, milk, juice, etc.)	235
Oils	215

GAS MARK	FAHRENHEIT	CELSIUS
1	275	140
2	300	150
3	325	165
4	350	175
5	375	190
6	400	200
7	425	220
8	450	230

GRAMS	OUNCES	GRAMS	OUNCES
10g	¼ oz	375g	13 oz
15g	½ oz	400g	14 oz
25g	1 oz	425g	15 oz
50g	1¾ oz	450g	1 lb
75g	2¾ oz	500g	1 lb 2 oz
100g	3½ oz	700g	1½ lb
150g	5½ oz	750g	1 lb 10 oz
175g	6 oz	1kg	2¼ lb
200g	7 oz	1.25kg	2 lb 12 oz
225g	8 oz	1.5kg	3 lb 5 oz
250g	9 oz	2kg	4½ lb
275g	9¾ oz	2.25kg	5 lb
300g	10½ oz	2.5kg	5½ lb
350g	12 oz	3kg	6½ lb